To Clift

Bless you.

Allan . P. Bell

27th July 2014

BREAKING THE CHAINS
OF MENTAL SLAVERY

Alton P. Bell

A & M PUBLISHING
LONDON

An imprint of
A & M Publishing
April Cottage, Ellis Avenue,
Chalfont Heights, Chalfont St Peter
Gerrards Cross, Bucks SL9 9UA
www.hdr-miniteries.co.uk

First Edition 2013
978 0 9574431 0 5

A catalogue record for this book is available
from the British Library

Typeset in Aldine401 BT
Printed and bound in UK
For Catbird Ltd, 26 Popin Business Centre
South Way, Wembley, Middlesex HA9 0HF

BREAKING THE CHAINS
OF MENTAL SLAVERY

Contents

ACKNOWLEDGEMENT

I would like to thank God for sending Jesus Christ into this world to become the curse for me so that  I can live and walk in the Blessing of Abraham. The fact that I accepted Jesus as my Lord and Saviour at an early age has been a life changing experience. It has also enhanced my appreciation of who I am and the purpose for which I have been called. Like a newborn baby, I spent my formative Christian years gleaning, digesting and reconciling information from those who were elders of the faith. My father, Allan , my mother, Myrtle, Bishop [Overseer] Charles Wright and all those who were members of the Assemblies of the First Born Church, Heath Road, Battersea, London who taught me the principles of respect and good manners, are my heroes.

I would also like to thank my wife, Marva, who has been a tower of strength over the years of our marriage. Her support has been a constant since our initial move to Luton, and later when the Lord spoke to me again about moving back to Harrow to work in the Sunday school being run by my mother. When again in 2002 the Lord spoke to me, firstly to run an Alpha Course, and then to study theology full time, she supported me.

I would also like to thank Mark Sturge for his friendship and support; Winston Bygrave for being there; Dr Anthony Reddie for his insight and wisdom in teaching me the tenets of Black theology and giving me a different perspective on my faith. I would like to thank all my brothers and sisters at Wembley Family Church who have walked the walk of faith with me and have accommodated me over the years.

Finally, I would like to thank my children for their love; it is because of them that I am now so passionate about removing the chains of mental slavery from those who have unwittingly been entangled by it. As you read this book may the light of the gospel of Jesus Christ enlighten your mind so that your transformation will be swift and painless.

Alton P Bell 2013

INTRODUCTION

My reasons for writing this book are to investigate the ongoing impact of African Chattel enslavement on the mindset of Black people. I want to focus on those of African Caribbean background, especially Christians, as I believe many still manifest slavery's negative traits and practices, even though they profess to have been changed by the 'blood of Jesus'. It is the insistence that we are 'saved', 'sanctified' and 'Holy Ghost baptised' but still ignorant of recent history and the ongoing struggles we face, that has prompted me to grapple with this topic.

Not everything coming out of Africa is negative. During the enslavement period, people from the Caribbean have been brainwashed to look at all aspects of African culture as negative. During the reconstruction period of the 19th century and the civil rights movement of the 1960s, people from the African Diaspora were encouraged to embrace everything African. I recognise that there are many positive aspects from Africa such as the many cures for ills and diseases using natural remedies.

As a Black man and a Christian, it is my desire that African Caribbean people are empowered so that they can find their 'true identity' and obtain deliverance from the pain and brutality of the past.

I contend that ignorance is not bliss and if we are ignorant of the reasons why syndromes like the 'strong Black woman syndrome', or 'the Black man fathering many children with different women and not supporting them', remain prevalent within our communities, we will never be able to address them. Henty Berry, speaking in the Virginia House of

Delegates in America in 1832, described the situation as it existed in many parts of the South, with the words: "We have, as far as possible, closed every avenue by which light may enter their (the slaves) minds. If we could extinguish the capacity to see the light, our work would be complete; they would then be on a level with the beasts of the field and we should be safe. I am not certain that we would not do it, if we could find out the process and that on the plea of necessity." Taken from; *Brown America, The story of a New Race*, Edwin R. Embree, The Viking Press, 1931.

The Judeo-Christian biblical narrative categorically states in 2 Corinthians 5:17 that 'I am a new creation' because I am in Christ. However, if I do not know who I am, or I have not been delivered from the generational issues of the past, then I will unknowingly carry the 'curse' and pass it on to future generations. Therefore, this book aims to encourage all African Caribbean people to 'be transformed' by the renewing of their minds.

Although our spiritual identity is in Christ, we need to know who we are since we are also located in a particular culture with a particular worldview, which are both alien and sometimes hostile to us as Christians and Black people.

What is African chattel slavery?

Slavery is a civil relationship whereby one person has absolute power over another and controls his or her life, liberty, and fortune. From antiquity, or as far back as we have records, individuals or specific people groupings have tried to exercise absolute power over others. People who are 'owned' by another are termed 'chattel slaves' since they are the property of that individual or family or nation. Using forced labour to build your house, city or country has been a long established practice in human history. The Egyptian dynasty, which was one of the first civilised societies, used chattel slaves to construct their edifices, landmarks and pyramids, many of which are still standing today.

The trade in people as slaves has a long history, and would require tomes of material to cover. However, the focus of this book is the trade in African people, and in particular the justification for moving millions of people from the continent of Africa to the Americas from the 15th century onwards. Before 1400, slavery had existed in Europe and did not disappear with the collapse of the Roman Empire. Slaves remained common in Europe throughout the early medieval period. However, chattel slavery of the classical type became increasingly uncommon in northern Europe by the 11th and 12th centuries. Nevertheless, forms of forced labour, such as villeinage and serfdom, persisted in the north well into the early modern period (1500-1800). In southern and eastern Europe, classical-style slavery remained a normal part of the society and the economy. However, trade across the Mediterranean and the Atlantic coastline meant that enslaved Africans began to appear in Italy, Spain, Southern France and Portugal well before the discovery of the so-called New World in 1492. An Arab-run slave trade also flourished from about the 8th century onwards, with much of this activity occurring in East Africa, Arabia and the Indian Ocean.

Additionally, many African societies practised forms of chattel slavery, although these differed considerably from the European and Arabic forms. Although various forms of coerced labour were prevalent in Europe throughout its history, historians refer to 'chattel slavery', as the term by which slaves were used as commodities to be bought and sold, rather than domestic servants or agricultural workers. Therefore, chattel slavery was the characteristic form of enslavement in the so-called modern world.

All the major European powers were involved in African chattel slavery at some stage. However, it was the Portuguese, who in 1441 were the first to start trading in Africans as slaves. A few years later, they began using enslaved Africans to cultivate sugar cane on the island of Maderia, off the cost of mainland Portugal. As these European colonialists became more and more adventurous, they sought different ways to increase their nation's gross domestic product (GDP). The financial profits from these new business ventures were so lucrative, that Pope Nicholas the V issued a Papal Bull in 1452 allowing the Portuguese to reduce all non-Christians to slaves. (A Papal Bull is the equivalent of an Act of Parliament. The head of the Roman Catholic Church is the Pope who has moral authority over all the countries in Europe whose state religion is Catholicism.) He followed this up in 1454 with a further Papal Bull granting the Portuguese a virtual monopoly in African chattel slavery. Once the coffers of the state and the church started to swell with the rewards of the slave trade, Portuguese Christians sought to develop theological arguments to justify the trade in Africans.

To validate the trade in African people and colonial expansion, Christian theology developed two principles; the first and most prominent was the theory of the Curse of Ham as depicted in Genesis 9:20-27. Here Noah curses Canaan the grandson of Ham and condemns him to a life of servitude. For these theologians, Ham signified the Black race, and consequently Black people or people with an African phenotype were deemed to be subservient. This principle lasted for several centuries and was used by the Dutch Reformed Church to sanction the South African Government to introduce Apartheid in 1948.

The second principle was the justification for colonialism and wars. Since evangelism was a central tenet in Christian doctrine, the colonialists used this as a means of bringing civilisation to the 'barbarians' and 'heathens' in Africa. With African chattel slavery now justified economically, politically and morally, the Spanish, French, British, Germans, Italians and the Dutch all partook in the trading of Africans.

The 'discovery' and colonisation of the Americas by the Italian explorer Christopher Columbus in 1492, eventually led to a great demand for human labour to produce goods for the increasingly modern countries of Western Europe. Over the next three centuries (1500-1800), statisticians estimate that more than 10million African men, women and children were forcibly taken to the west. This estimation excludes those who died in transit or those who were thrown overboard to reduce the tonnage on many slave ships. The manner of their transportation and the brutality that they faced when they arrived in the west was barbaric.

The Trans-Atlantic crossing, or 'Middle Passage', could take anywhere from six weeks to three months to complete. The Africans were stacked like' sardines' in the ships, since the more slaves delivered for sale, the more money the merchants and seafarers could make. Since the enslaved Africans were merchandise, they travelled naked, and the sailors would often rape the women, violate the men and subject others to horrendous torture whilst on these ships. On arrival in the west, the life expectancy of the average slave in the Caribbean was a meagre seven years. The Trans-Atlantic slave trade became a part of the 'Triangular Trade', which brought munitions to Africa, slaves to the Americas and produce such as sugar, cotton and spices to Europe.

The Portuguese, who started the African enslavement endeavour, built several slavery stations in the coastal areas of West Africa. The most notorious of these was Elmina Castle in modern-day Ghana, which still stands today. Here the Africans were put in shackles and chains, which is believed was made in foundries in Birmingham now the site of Cadbury's Chocolate, a Quaker company, and tethered to a wall or a post for several weeks; those who survived these horrendous conditions were shipped off to the Americas.

Over time, enslaved Africans would use a plethora of methods to help them survive, including insurrection and uprisings. Although Africans survived and produced offspring, the sheer barbarity of enslavement left an indelible scar on their psyche and that of their descendants. The Jamaican academic, Dr Orlando Patterson, in his book, *Slavery and Social Death* (1982), describes this form of slavery as 'social death' because it represents the permanent, violent domination of natally alienated and generally dishonoured persons who are subjected to violence, violation of personhood, dishonour and namelessness. Essentially this person has no rights, no place in society, no voice and therefore for all intents and purposes, is dead. And thus the Trans- Atlantic slave trade and the enslavement of African people have left a legacy of disenfranchised people who lost most of their connectivity to the past, and most of the true meaning of community and the ceremonial rites of passages that define adulthood.

Chapter 1
THE LONG ROAD TO EMANCIPATION

While the colonisation of the Americas, particularly by the Spanish, presented new opportunities for commerce, it also presented them with several practical headaches. In 1505 the Spanish began to cultivate sugarcane on the island of Hispaniola, in what is the modern-day Dominican Republic. Four years later in 1509, the governor of the Spanish empire in the Caribbean, Diego Colon, the son of Columbus, complained that the native indigenous slaves did not work hard enough. The following year, King Ferdinand of Spain, authorised the transportation of 50 enslaved Africans to work on the plantations. The need for a hardy labour force to work the newly discovered lands in the Caribbean, and those of North and South America, set the scene for the steady flow of African slaves to the Americas. In 1518 King Charles V of Spain granted Lorenzo de Gorrevod, his Flemish courtier, permission to transport 4,000 enslaved Africans to the Americas, and from this point onwards the Trans-Atlantic slave trade proliferated until its abolition in 19th century.

The British entered the lucrative slave business in 1562 during the reign of Queen Elizabeth 1, when an English sailor, John Hawkins, obtained 300 slaves from Sierra Leone in West Africa and sold them illegally to the Spanish in the West Indies. Hawkins made two further voyages over a six-year period capturing over 1200 Africans and selling them on. The English would eventually go on to capture and colonise many of the islands in the Caribbean, and as British settlements were established in the west, English slave ships would supply slaves to these colonies rather than selling them to the Dutch and Spanish. It is estimated that during the 245 years that elapsed between Hawkins's first trip and the abolition of the slave trade by Britain in 1807, over 10,000 journeys were made to Africa by British merchant ships for slaves. Moreover, British ships carried over 3.4 million Africans to the Americas. Only the Portuguese transported more enslaved Africans to west – primarily to Brazil, a country which now has the world's second largest African community after Nigeria.

The history of the Trans-Atlantic slave trade has largely ignored the role of the Africans who resisted enslavement, and fought to end the practice in various ways. The African freedom movement was active from the very beginning of chattel slavery. In his book, 'Blacks in bondage: the slaves who abolished slavery', the Jamaican academic, Richard Hart, describes how resistance took many forms, some individual and some collaborative. Africans resisted capture and imprisonment, attacked slave ships from the shore and engaged in shipboard revolts, fighting to free themselves and others. Sometimes pregnant women preferred abortion to bringing a child into slavery. On the plantations, resistance reduced profitability and enslaved Africans tried to slow down the pace of work through feigning illness or breaking tools. Others ran away whenever possible, escaping to South America, England or North America. Some, like the Maroons in Jamaica, escaped to the hills and mountains and formed guerrilla bands that attacked plantations. Regardless of the extent of the punishments, or how many harsh laws were passed to control them, enslaved Africans still rebelled.

Moreover, many Africans who gained their freedom worked with the abolitionists to end slavery. During the late 18th and early 19th centuries, the slave revolts grew bigger, as did the efforts of the European colonialists to suppress them. While many enslaved people were killed for rebelling, resistance to slavery continued; they made it clear that if they were not set free, they would free themselves. The earliest recorded slave rebellion occurred in Hispaniola, on the part which is modern day Haiti, in 1522. Over the next 300 years, there would be many mini uprisings and several major fully-blown rebellions; the most famous of which occurred in the late nineteenth century in St Dominigue, modern day Haiti. This rebellion was led by Toussaint L'Ouverture, a house slave who learnt to read and write. Merchants who hated slavery, but nonetheless profited from it, fuelled the French Revolution of 1789 in France. They made a compromise about the situation in St Dominigue, declaring that all the Africans should remain slaves but citizenship should be extended to Mulattos (mixed with one parent being Black and the other being White) who could prove that their father was French. The population at the time was 30,000 Whites, 40,000 Mulattos and 500,000 Africans. In total 400 Mulattos became citizens. This concession infuriated the planters and sowed the seeds of revolt among the Africans. In August 1791 the Africans slaughtered their masters, burned their mansions, and later took possession of the French half of the island. L'Ouverture had sought to negotiate with the planters to little effect, so his army defeated them using the slogan, 'liberty or death', and he became the de facto governor of St Dominigue. In 1793 the leftist revolutionary rulers of France, known as the Jacobins, issued a decree abolishing slavery. The British saw this as an opening to secure the most lucrative island in the Caribbean and sent a huge expedition to capture St Dominigue. Between 1794 and

1798, the British fought Toussaint L'Ouveture's army and lost more men in this escapade than they did in the famous Battle of Trafalgar in 1805 against Napoleon Bonaparte.

A change in administration in France led to the new leader Napoleon Bonaparte sending an army to re-institute slavery in St Dominigue. In the first six months of the expedition in 1802, the French lost more than 10,000 men, half to L'Ouverture's army and the other half to disease. In June 1802 the beleaguered French Generals offered Toussaint a treaty if he would appear in person to sign it. Although suspicious, he went to meet them and was duly captured and shipped off to France. Toussaint was kept in a cold prison where he eventually died, probably from pneumonia and hypothermia. However, his army fought on without him and ultimately defeated the French. On 1 January 1804, the victorious leaders changed the name of their island from St Dominigue to Haiti, the name the indigenous people called the country. Haiti became the first independently governed island in the Caribbean, and after the USA, the second country in the Americas to declare independence. However, after gaining its independence, Britain, France and the newly established United State of America refused to trade with Haiti, who went from being one of the richest countries in the Americas at that time, to one of the poorest in the world today.

Another significant slave revolt was that of the Maroons in Jamaica. During the British colonisation of Jamaica they tried relentlessly to capture and subjugate the Maroons, who used a variety of ancient African techniques to take on and defeat the British. Maroon resistance baffled the British forces to such an extent that they were forced to enter into an agreement with them in 1739 which allowed the Maroons to have their own territory called Accompong in the hills of St Elizabeth that they still occupy today. Accompong is located in one of the two areas where runaway slaves settled, originally with the indigenous Taíno people, and it was isolated enough to be safe, first from the Spanish and later from the British. The town of Accompong was named after the noted Maroon leader who was the brother of Quao, Cuffy, Johnny and Cudjoe, and their sister Nanny the famous leader, and currently Jamaica's only female national hero.

The justification of slavery by the British pro-slavery lobby

Those in Britain with a vested interest in maintaining slavery became great apologists for this exploitative practice. They argued:

That the trade was necessary to the success and wealth of Britain: The merchants and planters warned that abolition would mean ruin for Britain, as the whole economy would collapse. This argument was put forward many times, for example, in 1749, when a pamphlet was written outlining these arguments.

If Britain did not engage in the trade then others would: If Britain ceased to trade in slaves with Africa, its commercial rivals, the French and the Dutch, would soon 'fill the gap' and the Africans would be in a much worse situation. This was an argument used in a speech to Parliament in 1777.

Africa was already involved in slavery: It was stated that Africans enslaved each other. Indeed, Britain was engaged in a moral trade because it was helping those captured in African wars who may otherwise have been executed.

Taking Africans from their homeland actually benefited them: It was argued that African societies and cultures were unskilled, uneducated and savage. For example, Michael Renwick Sergant, a merchant from Liverpool claimed: 'We ought to consider whether the negroes in a well regulated plantation, under the protection of a kind master, do not enjoy as great, nay, even greater advantages than when under their own despotic governments' – from 'the history of the British West Indies' (published 1819).

The enslaved people were unfit for other work: Many people were very prejudiced in their beliefs. The average Briton at that time was uneducated and travelled little further than their own village, making it easier for those involved in the slave trade to influence public opinion.

The enslaved people were not ill-treated unless rebellious, and conditions on - board the slave ships were acceptable: Several of those involved in the trade such as merchants, ships' captains and plantation owners, provided evidence to Parliament regarding this. One example is the report of Mr Norris to the Privy Council in 1789.

Slavery was accepted in the Bible. The pro-slavery supporters used verses from the Bible to suggest that the slave trade was approved by God in the days of Abraham. In 1788, the Revd Raymond Harris, a former Catholic priest and ardent slavery apologist, wrote the best selling publication "Scriptural researches on the licitness of the slave trade." which skilfully used scriptural verses to justify African slavery and to counter arguments from the British anti-slavery lobby.

The Anti-Slavery lobby developed arguments to counter African enslavement such as:

If something is wrong, it is wrong whether others do it or not: The anti-slavery supporters argued that just because other countries engaged in the Trade it did not provide a valid reason for Britain to also participate, even if it was profitable. This argument was used by Baron Grenville in his speech to the House of Lords when he said, "...Can there be a question that the character of the country ought to be cleared from the stain impressed by the guilt of such traffic..." The argument was also cleverly countered in William Cowper's poem 'A Pity for Poor Africans'.

The slavery that existed in Africa was very different from the Trans-Atlantic slave trade: Those enslaved in Africa were usually prisoners of war or victims of political or judicial punishment. They could keep their name and identity, and slavery did not extend to future generations.

The African people were in no way inferior and should be treated as equals: The Quaker teacher and abolitionist, Anthony Benezet, was always horrified at the suggestion that the Africans were in any way inferior. He claimed his experiences, gained during 20 years teaching Black pupils proved this was not the case. However, it was the books and speeches of African writers of the time, such as Olaudah Equiano that had the greatest impact in dispelling such misconceptions. Even some of those involved in the slave trade were willing to admit that racist views were wrong, as illustrated by the writings of Captain Thomas Philips.

The trade was damaging to Africa: The British MP and leading abolitionist, William Wilberforce, summed this up in his speech of 1789: "...Does anyone suppose a slave trade would help their civilization? Is it not plain, that she must suffer from it?....Does not everyone see that a slave trade, carried on around her coasts, must carry violence and desolation to her very centre?... Does the king of Barbess want brandy? He has only to send his troops in the night time, to burn and desolate a village; the captives will serve as commodities that may be bartered with the British trader."

The Africans suffered greatly from being removed from their homeland: The abolitionists collected evidence to show that many Africans resisted or preferred death to transportation. Many more died on the voyage to the Americas as the conditions on board the ships were terrible, as illustrated through the testimonies of abolitionists such as the former ship's doctor James Ramsay. The replacement rate statistics also showed the appallingly low life expectancy of Africans on the plantations (7-9 years on some large plantations).

It was morally wrong and, as a Christian country, Britain should not be involved: The anti-slavery society also used the Bible to back up their arguments by pointing to biblical texts like Luke 16:13: "No man can serve two masters". In answer to the claims of the pro-slavery lobby, the abolitionist Granville Sharp, for example, wrote in his pamphlet 'The just limitation of slavery in the Laws of God': "...If we carefully examine the scriptures we shall find that slavery and oppression were ever abominable in the sight of God..."

There were alternatives to the trade: Much of the evidence that the British abolitionist Thomas Clarkson collected during his travels illustrated the potential for practical alternatives to the slave trade. The seeds, minerals and crafts that he carried in 'the Clarkson box' were used to demonstrate this.

Other factors that led to the abolition of the Trans-Atlantic slave trade

There were many factors that led to the abolition of the slave trade, and later to slavery itself. As the Africans on the plantations in the Caribbean became literate, they used a variety of methods to reduce the productivity of the plantations, despite the harsh treatments of the planters and their Mulatto overseers or Backra's. These people were called 'Backra' (back raw) because it was they who would beat the slaves until their backs were bleeding and hence was raw.

When the USA became independent in 1776, Britain's major sugar colonies such as Jamaica and Barbados productivity declined, as the USA could trade directly with the French and Dutch in the West Indies. Furthermore, as the Industrial Revolution took hold in the 18th century, Britain no longer needed slave-produced goods. Cotton, rather than sugar, became the main produce of the British economy and English towns, such as Manchester and Salford, became industrial centres for their production.

Moreover, the slave revolts caused the plantation owners to reconsider their positions, as property and profits were severely affected. The Haitian rebellion in 1791 was followed by revolts in Barbados (1816), Demerara in modern day Guyana (1823) and Jamaica (1831-1832). Although the vast majority of the uprisings were quelled, the writing was on the wall for plantation slavery. The revolts also shocked the British government and made them see that the costs and dangers of keeping slavery in the West Indies were too high. In places like Jamaica, many terrified plantation owners were finally ready to accept abolition rather than risk a widespread war. And the rise of political activists and ex-slaves who were telling their stories of the horrors of the slave trade, were further nails in the coffin of the trade. Christian ministers, many of whom were from the nonconformist denominations, outlined the moral and ethical positions against slavery. Therefore, by the beginning of the nineteenth century not only was the industrial climate changing, but also the political and moral climate.

The British abolitionists took the view that if they went for the wholesale abolition of slavery, then it may take a long time, since there were many powerful figures in the pro-slavery lobby in the Houses of Parliament and the Lords. The first Bill put to Parliament in 1791 was rejected by 163 votes to 88. In 1793, Britain went to war against France. The Slave Trade was seen as the "nursery of seamen" and to oppose it seemed unpatriotic to many. Therefore, attention was diverted away from the abolition of slavery to the abolition of the trade. However, William Wilberforce continued to propose legislation for abolition in the House of Commons.

It was not until 1807, when the evils of the trade were generally accepted, that the law was able to pass both Houses. The first breakthrough occurred in 1806, when a Bill written by James Stephen was passed, banning involvement in the slave trade with France. Other events played a part too. The Act of Union allowed 100 Irish MPs into Parliament, most of whom supported abolition. The chances of abolition became even more favourable when William (Lord) Grenville, who was extremely sympathetic to the views of the anti-slavery committee, became Prime Minister after the death of William Pitt.

The effect of Stephen's 1806 Act was to reduce the trade by two-thirds, thus paving the way for the Abolition of the Slave Trade Act in February 1807. The Prime Minister, Lord Grenville, introduced the Slave Trade Abolition Bill in the House of Lords on the 2 January 1807 where it received a first reading. The House of Lords voted for the abolition of the slave trade on 5 February by 100 votes to 34 after an impassioned speech by the Prime Minister, despite opposition from the West India Lobby. The Bill was debated for 10 hours in the House of Commons on 23rd February. At 4am, the next morning the House voted in favour of the Bill by 283 votes to 16. Finally, on 25 March 1807 the Abolition of the Slave Trade Act received its royal assent, abolishing the slave trade in the British colonies and making it illegal to carry enslaved people in British ships.

Parliamentary reform

The demand for freedom for enslaved people had become almost universal. It was now driven forward, not only by the formal abolition campaign but also by a coalition of non-conformist churches, as well as evangelicals in the Church of England. When Parliament was finally reformed in 1832, two-thirds of those who supported slavery were swept from power. The once powerful West India Lobby had lost its political strength.

In July 1833, a Bill to abolish slavery throughout the British Empire was passed in the House of Commons, followed by the House of Lords on 1 August. The Act, however, did not free enslaved people immediately - they were to become "apprentices" for 6 years. (Only Antigua gave the Africans full freedom at this juncture.) The British Government promised compensated the planters to the tune of £20 million pounds, which was 40 per cent of the country's GDP at the time and the equivalent of £17 billion pounds in today's money. Conversely, the 700,000 Africans in the British Caribbean received a yard (3 square feet) of land to cultivate and survive on. Protests finally forced the government to abolish the apprenticeship system and on 1 August 1838, all enslaved African people in the British Empire were technically free.

Chapter 2

FREE AT LAST!

The abolition of the slave trade and chattel slavery did not bring self-governance to the colonies. In the first instance, the vast majority of the former slave population were illiterate and only trained to work on sugar, coffee and banana plantations. During centuries of slavery, it was illegal to teach Africans to read and write and they were prohibited from getting married. Enslaved Africans were 'bred' like animals to provide cheap labour for the prosperous plantations on the Caribbean islands of Antigua and Barbuda in particular.

The road towards self-governance would be long and arduous, and would eventually mirror the fate suffered by Haiti. As the only Black self-governing nation in the Americas, Haiti found that all her European controlled neighbours wanted to control her and thus have access to the prosperous Caribbean island. This resulted in these countries, many of them natural rivals, conspiring to alienate and destroy Haiti. There is ample historical evidence which shows that Haiti's independence was a threat to an aggressive North-Atlantic alliance that could not imagine their world inhabited by free Africans running a newly emerging democracy.

The popular perception is that somehow the Haitian nation-building project, launched on 1 January 1804, failed because of mismanagement, ineptitude and corruption, nothing could be further from the truth. The Haitians fought for their freedom and won, as did the Americans some 30 years earlier. The Americans declared their independence and crafted an extraordinary constitution that set out a clear message about the value of humanity and the right to freedom, justice, and liberty. In the midst of this brilliant discourse, they chose to retain slavery as the basis of the new nation state. The Founding Fathers could not see beyond race, as they built the free United States on the foundation of slavery. Once the Americans realised that slavery and freedom could not comfortably co-exist in the same place, they went back to the battlefield a century later to resolve this issue.

Equally, the French declared freedom, fraternity and equality as the new philosophies of their national transformation and gave the modern world a tremendous progressive boost by so doing. They abolished slavery but Napoleon Bonaparte could not imagine the Republic without enslavement and targeted the Haitians for a new, more intense regime of slavery. The British agreed, as did the Dutch, Spanish and Portuguese since all wanted to get their hands on the jewel of the Caribbean. The French refused to recognise Haiti's independence and declared it an illegal pariah state. The Americans, whom the Haitians looked to in solidarity as their mentor in independence, refused to recognise them, and offered solidarity instead to the French. The British, who were negotiating with the French to obtain the ownership title to Haiti, also moved in solidarity, as did every other nation-state the western world.

As mentioned previously, the Haitians won a ten-year war, which was one of the bloodiest in modern history, and subsequently declared their independence. At the time, every other country in the Americas had a slave-based system, which was in stark contrast to Haiti, whose 1805 Independence Constitution stated that any person of African descent who arrived on its shores would be declared free, and a citizen of the Republic. History reveals that Haiti was isolated at birth, ostracised and denied access to world trade, finance and institutional development – this was the most vicious example of national strangulation recorded in modern history. The Haitians were alone from inception and the crumbling soon began.

In 1825 the Republic marked its 21st anniversary with great festivities, but there was little to celebrate as the economy was bankrupt and the political leadership isolated. The Haitian Cabinet took the decision to find a way back into the world economy and invited the French government to a summit. When the French officials arrived they told the Haitians that they were only willing to recognise the country as a sovereign nation if it agreed to pay reparations for loss of earnings over the 21-year period. The Haitians, with their backs against the wall, agreed to pay the French. The French government sent a team of accountants and actuaries to Haiti in order to place a value on all lands, physical assets, the 500 000 citizens were who formerly enslaved (this included members of the Haitian Cabinet), animals, and all other commercial properties and services. The sums amounted to 150 million gold Francs, and Haiti was forced to pay this reparation to France in return for national recognition. Thus began the systematic destruction of the Republic of Haiti which the French government bled and rendered it a failed state. Haiti took one hundred years to pay off this sum – they finished paying it in 1922 when they made the final instalment. During the 19th century the payment amounted to more than 70 per cent of the country's foreign exchange earnings, landing the country into financial and social chaos.

On the other hand, France was enriched by the payments and took pleasure from the fact that although they were defeated by Haitians on the battlefield, they won on the field of finance. In the years when their crops failed, the Haitian government borrowed on the French money market at double the going interest rate in order to repay the French government. When the Americans invaded the country in the early 20th century, one of the reasons offered was to assist the French in collecting its reparations.

Although strong representation has been made to the French government to repay the 150 million Francs, to date they have not repaid a Franc. The estimated current value of the money paid to France is US$21 billion. If France were to repay this money it would go some way toward releasing Haiti from the shackles of financial poverty and set them free at last.

The British colonies such as Jamaica and Barbados were governed from Westminster, in London, with a local governor in place. The British instituted a very rigid class system based on skin pigmentation. The fraternisation of merchants and planters with the enslaved Africans produced a Brown middle class called Mulattoes. In this new post-slavery society, people were categorised according to their colour, and there was a wide range of colours in this colonial pigmentocratic elitist system, with those who were White at the top of society and those who were Black at the bottom. Those who were Mulatto, Quadroon or Octoroon shared the middle tiers. In all, there were about 13 different colour gradations.

Educating the ex-slave community

If those from these ex-slave communities wanted to assume governance of their islands, they had to be educated to function. Yet, education had largely been forbidden in slave-based colonies. Of all the reformed Christian denominations that existed in the Caribbean colonies, the Moravians were the first to work among the slave community, teaching them to read and write and instructing them on the true tenets of the Good News of Jesus.

The Moravian missionary movement was founded in 1722 at Herrnhut, near Dresden in Saxony, Germany by a Lutheran priest, Count Nikolaus von Zinzendorf. He offered part of his estate as a refuge to a group of persecuted believers from Bohemia and Moravia. These 'Brethren' at Herrnhut started a 24-hour prayer movement, which lasted for over 100 years. They began the first organised Protestant mission by sending missionaries all over the world to preach and live out the gospel of Jesus. When these missionaries left Herrnhut, they took all their belongings in a coffin, knowing that they would never return. The Moravians were so committed to spreading the gospel that two German missionaries made themselves slaves in their attempt to reach the African slave community. Despite opposition from the planters and the possibility of death from disease, they established a mission in Danish St Thomas in 1732. This was followed by a mission in the British colonial region of Demerara, modern day Guyana in 1738, Jamaica in 1754, Antigua in 1756 and Barbados in 1765. Other Protestant denominations copied the Moravian's model and participated in the education of the slave communities in the Americas and in Africa.

Education for liberation?

Several factors compounded the education of the ex-slave community in the Caribbean. The principle one was the way several generations of enslavement had affected the psyche of the people, which led to identity issues. Were these people African, West Indian or some new hybrid nation? Many of the Africans who fought and defeated their European captors, such as the Maroons and the Haitians, maintained and practised rituals and customs learned on the continent of Africa. This was in spite of the colonialists' best effort to destroy the language and culture of enslaved people. There is little doubt that there was a definite plan to create a 'disconnect' between the enslaved Africans on the plantations and any notions of their African heritage. Although the vast majority of Africans were given Christian names on arrival in the west, many of their former practices were inter-mingled with the Christianity they practised, which created its own problems. To this day many people in the Caribbean, Jamaicans in particular, have two names - one for the 'yard', a judging name, and another for 'abroad', a dressing name.

Nonetheless, the vast majority of those who were enslaved were Creoles; people who were born in the Caribbean but whose ancestry came from different parts of Africa. Others were the product of relationships between African women and European men - often the result of rape. As a result of miscegenation, many people from the Caribbean have more European than African blood in their genetic make-up. After emancipation in 1838, the influx of Indians as indentured servants and then the Chinese caused further intermingling to occur. In addition, since the Africans could not choose their partners, women often had children by multiple partners and as soon as young girls began menstruating, they would be impregnated either by the plantation owners or by those in positions of authority on the plantations. Their policy was, 'if you bleed', you can breed.

There was also a deliberate colonial policy of 'divide and rule' by locating people in society according to the shade of their skin tone, to create mistrust, fear and envy amongst the slave community. The colonialists maintained the status quo by teaching the slave community to discriminate against one another because of skin colour, hair texture, the shape of one's nose, and the work carried out on the plantation etc. This also led to the perception that being Black meant being inferior, bad and subversive, while White was good. Such ideas became deeply ingrained in the language, culture and psyche of the Victorian colonialists.

Although the evangelistic zeal of Moravians helped in the education of the ex-slave community, the vast majority remained illiterate and would not be in a position to partake in any form of democracy for another one hundred years. The socio-economic status of the freed Caribbean individual was still precarious. After having served several years of apprenticeship for their former masters, many ended up working as peons, living from hand to mouth to survive and unable to forward plan.

Chapter 3

ACTIVISM, VERBALISM AND CONSCIENTISATION!

The legacy of slavery and post-colonialism condemned generations of Black people to live in denial of their Blackness and their culture. Generations of Black people lived in parallel worlds without coming to a conclusion about where they should or could plant themselves. At the turn of the twentieth century Black educators and conscious Black people started to reflect on the Black experience as a means of self-affirmation and a tool for Black religious education.

Because of the ravages of slavery, the term Black, or Negro, was used to describe people of African origin. However, it must be borne in mind that Africa is not a country, but a continent with different countries each having their own culture, traditions and mores. The concept of Black took on political connotations, and became a source of pride and identity with the rise of activists in the twentieth century who challenged the modernist notions that associated everything negative with a 'black' prefix. So, economists, scientist and anthropologists from previous centuries coined terms such as "Black Monday' a time when there was a crisis in the world's economy, 'Black hole', a phenomenon coined by scientists to describe a state where nothing can escape; and 'Black list', which is a list of people who cause subterfuge and are therefore anti-establishment.

At the beginning of the twentieth century, there were contrasting views among Black intellectuals and activists within the Black community on how to deal with the problem of racism and White hegemony. (It is ironic that at the beginning of the twenty-first century the Black community is still concerned about the progress of a vast majority of its constituents, particularly its young adolescent males.)

Black people such as the African American Fredrick  Douglass (1818-1895), an abolitionist, orator, author, editor and reformer, reflected on the barbarity of slavery, the dichotomy of the religious slave holders in the southern states of America and the need for active agitation against a corrupt system. He stated: "The whole history of the progress of human liberty, shows that all concessions yet made to her august claims have been born of earnest struggle. If there is no struggle, there is no progress. Those who profess to favour freedom, and yet deprecate agitation, are men who want crops without ploughing up the ground. They want rain without thunder and lightning. They want the ocean without the awful roar of its many waters. This struggle may be a moral one; or it may be a physical one; or it may be both moral and physical; but it must be a struggle. Power concedes nothing without a demand. It never did and it never will. Find out just what a people will submit to, and you have found out the exact amount of injustice and wrong, which will be imposed upon them; and these will continue until they are resisted with either words or blows, or with both. The limits of tyrants are prescribed by the endurance of those whom they oppress." (Taken from an address to West India Emancipation on 3rd August 1857).

Douglass also made some insightful comments about the dichotomy of the southern slave owners who reportedly practised their religion, yet justified the appalling barbarity and inhumane treatment of their enslaved Africans. Douglass was born a slave and asserted that the religion of the south was a covering for the barbarity they inflicted on their prize possession, the Africans.

The conscientisation of the freedman was now the pressing business for intelligent Black activists. We can define conscientisation as the *"iconic representations that have a powerful emotional impact in the daily lives of learners. In this way, individual consciousness helps end the "culture of silence" in which the socially dispossessed internalize the negative images of themselves created and propagated by the oppressor in situations of extreme poverty. Liberating learners from this* mimicry *of the powerful, and the fratricidal violence that results from this, is a major goal of critical consciousness. Succinctly put, conscientisation is consciousness raising to the point of critical consciousness where the learner questions the nature of their historical and social condition and seeks to democratise them"*.

One of the first tasks for the conscientised Black person was to rebuild the family unit and re-institute the societal order as depicted in the Judeo-Christian creation narrative of Genesis 2:24. Prior to emancipation, marriage among enslaved Africans was illegal and as far as Douglass was concerned, slavery had done away with fathers and did not recognise the existence of families in its social arrangements on the plantations.

It can be argued that there were three key stalwarts of the Black community who being conscientised, used their methods and the resources available to them to change the lot of their communities. Their drive to help educate and thus raise the ability of the Black individual to be more than farmers and peons was driven by their understanding of the

Christian gospel and the God of the Bible who always seem to be on the side the poor, marginalised and oppressed.

The first person was Booker T. Washington, an African-American who was born before the abolition of slavery in the USA in 1863. Washington worked within the racist system in America to raise the level of education among his people.

Booker T Washington

In his autobiography Booker T. (Taliaferro) Washington states that he was born as a slave in Franklyn County, Virginia between 1858/59. He gained his freedom when slavery was abolished after the American Civil War (1861-1865). During his early years after freedom, the ex-slaves were deliberately kept uneducated to provide a readily available workforce for the plantations, factories and farms in the southern states of America. It was whilst working in a salt furnace in West Virginia with his stepfather, and in a local coalmine that Booker T. Washington developed a yearning to learn to read and the need to educate himself. His story is one of him literally pulling himself up by his bootstraps to become over time an influential leader of his community. He developed a non-confrontational stance in the quest to uplift his race.

Although Washington was born into slavery to a White father he never knew and an African-American slave mother whom he adored, as a young man he worked in West Virginia in a variety of manual jobs before making his way to a Negro Institute in Hampton, seeking an education. He worked his way through Hampton Agricultural Institute (now Hampton University) and later attended college at Wayland Seminary. This college was established in 1865 by the American Baptist Home Mission Society primarily to provide education and training for African-American freedmen to enter into the ministry. He argued that the Black community should work with those in the White community who were willing to work for the benefit of the wider Black community. He gained access to top national leaders in politics, philanthropy and education and used these connections to further his own institute at Tuskegee. Washington's efforts included cooperating with White people and enlisting the support of wealthy philanthropists, who helped him raise funds to establish and operate thousands of small community schools and institutions of higher education for the uplifting of Black people throughout the South of America.

Washington had high aspirations for his "Negro race". The basis of his theory was this: by providing needed skills to society, African Americans would play a full part in society, leading to acceptance by their White peers. He believed that Black people should not seek social change until they had raised their economic status, and would eventually gain full participation in society by showing themselves to be responsible, reliable American citizens. Although this line of argument is plausible, he was trying to redress an imbalance that was over three hundred years in the making and this stance totally omitted the conditions of Black people in other parts of the world. Washington was passionate about working within the system to effect change and believed that this could only be achieved by economic means. During his famous "Atlanta compromise speech" in 1895 Washington soothed his listeners' concerns about "uppity" Black people by claiming that his "race" would content itself with living "by the productions of our hands".

While Washington was seen as the leader of the Negro Race and his plans were plausible, he never made an attempt in all his endeavours to address the social inequality that existed, particularly among his Black people and the dominant White community. Nor did he address the Jim Crow laws that prevented Black people from using certain public places - staying in hotels or riding anywhere on public transport. Washington's stance of working in the background to effect change opened many doors for him but brought him into confrontation with others from the Black community who saw him as seemingly supporting the status quo of 'separate but equal' that the Southern States made law in 1876. Although White society regarded him as the official spoke person for African Americans, and he later became an advisor to several Presidents, others within the African American community such as W.E.B. Du Bois criticised him for not challenging or fighting for greater social change. Washington's stance at the time was understandable since in his eyes, to go from a slave to a position of elected office, when the majority of your people could not read let alone vote, was real progress.

Although Washington made great strides in acquiring buildings and setting up institutes to help his people, by not fighting for social justice and equality, structural racism remained untouched in America during his lifetime. Today in Britain Washington is virtually unknown by the Black community.

W. E. B Du Bois

The next stalwart of the Black community was William Edward Burghardt (W.E.B.) Du Bois who took a more radical stance against White hegemony. W.E.B Du Bois was a prominent thinker and writer at the turn of the 20th century.

 He has authored several books; his most seminal work was *The Souls of Black Folks*, New York: Bantam Books, 1969, in which he advocated his most famous term of 'double consciousness'. Unlike Washington, Du Bois was born just after the end of the American Civil War on 23 February 1868 in Great Barrington, Massachusetts, U.S.A. He grew up in the period known as the 'Reconstruction' when many of the rights and privileges of citizenship were being realised by the African American population. Du Bois was fortunate enough to know his mother and father, however soon after he was born his parent's relationship fell apart, and his father left the family to live in New York. Du Bois grew up with his mother and other family members from his mother's side. His mother carried out menial jobs to support the family, but her ill health meant that she could not command a worthwhile salary to educate him and house the family. She recognised that young Du Bois was bright and that education was a route for him out of poverty.

In Great Barrington, he did not face overt racism. He was one of only a handful of Black students to graduate from high school since at the time many would only learn to read, write and leave to learn a 'trade'. After graduating from high school, Du Bois wanted to continue his studies at university, however he faced the problem of how to fund this ambition. He particularly wanted to attend Harvard, due to its reputation and its proximity, but failed to obtain a place at the university because of his colour and the poor standard of education he had received from his high school.

While visiting his grandfather in New York he experienced the richness and diversity of Black culture in the city, and these experiences would have a great influence on him later in his life. They would also lay the foundations for a lifetime of arguing, agitating and campaigning for civil liberties. His local headmaster arranged a package along with other prominent member of his local community to provide support for him so that he could attend university. Therefore, in the autumn of 1885 the 17 year old Du Bois was packed off to attend a Black institution in Nashville, Tennessee called Fisk University. It was whilst attending this Tennessee university that he witnessed firsthand the appalling treatment of Black people in the South.

Du Bois graduated from Fisk in 1888. He continued his studies at Harvard where in 1895 he became the first Black man to graduate with a PhD. His doctoral dissertation, *The Suppression of the African Slave-Trade to the United States of America, 1638–1870*, was published the following year. Du Bois was broadly trained in the social sciences and, at a time when other sociologists were theorising about race relations, he was conducting empirical inquiries into the condition of Black folks, not just in America but in far flung places around the world. He would visit many of these countries later in his life. For more than a decade, Du Bois devoted himself to sociological investigations of Blacks in America, producing 16 research monographs published between 1897 and 1914 at Atlanta Georgia University, where he obtained a chair. He was the first academic to empirically study Black communities in the United States and in 1899 he published a first ever-case study entitled *The Philadelphia Negro: A Social Study*.

Although Du Bois had originally believed that social science could provide the knowledge to solve the race problem, he gradually concluded that in a climate of virulent racism, expressed in such evils as lynching, peonage, disfranchisement, Jim Crow segregation laws and race riots, social change would only come through agitation and protest. This viewpoint clashed with the most influential Black leader of the period, Booker T. Washington, who, preaching a philosophy of accommodation, urged Black folks to accept discrimination while seeking to elevate themselves through hard work and economic gain. In 1903, Du Bois seminal *The Souls of Black Folk* charged that Washington's strategy, rather than freeing the Black man from oppression, would serve only to perpetuate it. This attack crystallized the opposition to Washington among many Black intellectuals, polarizing the leaders of the Black community into two wings—the "conservative" supporters of Washington and the "radical" critics led by Du Bois.

Du Bois held posts at other universities but it was as a co-founder of the National Association for the Advancement of Coloured People (NAACP) in 1909, which is still active today, for which he is best known. He used his position as editor of the 'Crisis' (1910 -1934), the mouthpiece of the NAACP, to galvanise both progressive White sympathisers and middle class Black people. He argued vehemently that the Black community was involved in a struggle for self-identification and out of necessity should move beyond complicity with the White community as advocated by Washington. Consequently, he introduced the concept of 'double consciousness' which he defined as, *"the sense of looking at one's self through the eyes of others, of measuring one's soul by the tape of a world that looks on in amused contempt and pity, two warring ideals in one dark body, whose dogged strength alone keeps it from being torn asunder."* He stressed the need to remove the dichotomy of double consciousness, which denied Black self-identity. Since the White community revelled in the promotion of oppression for the Black community, Black people should struggle to move beyond oppression towards self-worth and self-identity. He again clashed with Washington over the education of Black youngsters, and argued that Black people should study academic subjects rather than training to be farmers and factory workers. He asserted that since the Reconstruction, political power, the insistence on civil rights and higher education of 'Negro Youth' should be 'a given'. One of his most controversial proposals was the institution of the 'Talented Tenth' which involved selecting the top ten per cent from the Black population and ensuring that they were the recipients of the best education. Du Bois never gave details of how this would work, but as an academic idealist he knew the benefits of a good education.

Many of the civil rights that Du Bois agitated for became law under President Lyndon Johnson, the year after his death in August 1963. Du Bois was instrumental in conscientising the Black community to agitate for social justice, and his ideas would be picked up by other prominent Black activists.

Marcus Mosiah Garvey

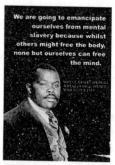

The third and most radical activist was Marcus Garvey who rejected the 'White world' and actively promoted a Black one as an alternative. Marcus Mosiah Garvey was born in the parish of St Ann, Jamaica as a British citizen on 17 August 1887. He was a descendant of the Maroon people and from the age of 14 he worked as a printer in the capital, Kingston. Even at this early age, he started agitating for better working conditions and privileges for his fellow Black workers. Garvey left Jamaica for Costa Rica in 1910 where he worked as a timekeeper on a banana plantation while staying with an uncle. As he observed the conditions under which his fellow Black workers laboured, he became determined to change the lives of his people. In referring to God's relationship with humanity, Garvey wrote: "When God breathed into the nostrils of man the breath of life, He made him a living soul, and bestowed upon him the authority of "Lord of Creation." He never intended that an individual should descend to the level of a peon, a serf, or a slave, but that he should be always man in the fullest possession of his senses and with the truest knowledge of himself, but how changed has man become since creation? We find him today divided into different classes — the helpless imbecile, the dependant slave, the servant and master. These different classes God never created. He created man".

Garvey left Costa Rica and travelled throughout Central America, working and observing the conditions of Black folks in the region. His travels throughout the region included Guatemala, Panama, Nicaragua, Bocas-del-Toro, Ecuador, Chile, and Peru. He found West Indian workers experiencing great hardships in all of these Spanish-speaking republics. Most had left their overpopulated Caribbean islands because of unemployment and poverty. In 1912, Garvey left Jamaica and sailed to England, where his only surviving sister, Indiana, lived. It was in London that he learned about African culture and became interested in the conditions of Blacks in the United States. Garvey began taking part in the 'free-for-all' at Speaker's Corner in London's Hyde Park. He was also a regular visitor at the House of Commons, spent large amounts of time in the reading rooms at the British Library and attended lectures at Birkbeck College. At the same time, Garvey befriended Duse Muhammad, an Egyptian nationalist who published a paper called *The African and Orient Review*. It was through his friendship with Muhammad that he gained an international perspective on the struggles of African people throughout the world.

While in London, Garvey also read Booker T. Washington's autobiography and other works by the American activist and educator. Garvey wrote, "I read of conditions in America. I read *Up From Slavery*, and then my doom — if I may so call it — of being a race leader dawned upon me." Although it had been over four decades since the abolition of slavery in the United States, many still considered Black people as the inferior race. Garvey began to ask unanswerable questions: "Where is the Black man's government? Where is his king and kingdom? Where is his President, his country and ambassador, his army, his navy, his men of big affairs? I will help to make them," he declared and with that, he headed home to Jamaica.

Garvey returned to Jamaica in 1914 with a vision to establish an organisation to "unite all Negro peoples in the world into one great body to establish a country and government that was absolutely their own". Booker T. Washington's philosophy of self-improvement for people of African descent had influenced him greatly during his voyage back home, and five days after his arrival, the Universal Negro Improvement Association and African Communities League were born. Garvey was later to state: "Such a name I thought would embrace the purpose of all Black humanity. Thus to the world a name was born, a movement created, and a man became known." The organisation declared its motto — *One God! One Aim! One Destiny!*

The following year at the age of 28, Garvey migrated to the USA and settled in Harlem, New York. Here, his ideas expanded and he became a Black Nationalist. For him, Africa was the ancestral home and the spiritual base for all people of African descent and his political goal was to take Africa back from European domination and build a free and united

Black Africa. He advocated the 'Back-to-Africa Movement' and organized a shipping company called the *Black Star Line* which was part of his programme to conduct international trade between Black Africans and the rest of the world. Garvey hoped this would "uplift the race" and eventually see the return of all Africans to Africa.

To publicise the U.N.I.A. he founded a weekly newspaper called *'The Negro World'* in 1918 which was published in French, Spanish and English. Garvey glorified African history and its heroes and declared himself the "Provisional President of Africa". Despite the lack of consultation with any native Africans, both he and the members of his "empire" would parade in elaborate military uniforms during their annual conventions in Harlem. Over a short space of time, delegates from all over the United States, the Caribbean, Central America and Africa would attend his conventions. Garvey travelled throughout the United States speaking and meeting with African American leaders. In post World War I America with racial discrimination, lynching and poor housing, the masses of Black people were ready for a leader who was aggressive and had a plan to "uplift the race". The U.N.I.A. grew quickly and by 1919 there were over 30 branches throughout the United States, the Caribbean, Latin America and Africa. Garvey claimed that over a million people had joined his organisation in three years. In nine years, Garvey built the largest mass movement of people of African descent in America's history.

Garvey's business efforts in Harlem were under constant surveillance by the Bureau of Investigation who looked for any opportunity to arrest him. Garvey's movement began to fail after he was convicted of mail fraud and gaoled in 1922. He spent four months in a New York prison, but after representing himself and arguing his case, he was subsequently released. A full two years later, in 1925, he was re-arrested and sent to prison in Atlanta, Georgia, where he served a two-year gaol sentence. On release, the U.S.A. deported him to Jamaica in 1927.

Once back in Jamaica, Garvey worked hard to rebuild the U.N.I.A. and travelled extensively. He visited many branches of the organisation in other West Indian territories and in Central America. In 1928, Garvey left Jamaica for Europe, where he wanted to establish his European headquarters, and carried out a speaking tour of Britain, France, Belgium, Germany and Switzerland. His attempt to visit Canada was thwarted as he was detained in Montreal and deported once again to Jamaica.

In 1929, Garvey founded the People's Political Party, Jamaica's first modern political party, which included such goals as a larger share of self-government, protection for native industries and a legal aid department for the poor. Garvey's return to Jamaica, which also saw him move the U.N.I.A.'s headquarters to the island, caused widespread fragmentation and desertion among branches in the United States. Although the U.N.I.A.'s 1929 convention in Kingston was able to recapture some of the splendour and enthusiasm of the early Harlem era, the organisation never amassed a substantial membership again.

In 1931, Garvey launched the Edelweiss Amusement Company in Jamaica which exemplified the necessity for artists to make a living from their work. The majority of the entertainment was based on church, school and folk entertainment, and Garvey wrote plays and poems for presentation. On Sundays Garvey conducted a non-denominational, religious service for attendees.

In 1935, Garvey migrated to London and in 1937 began the publication of a series of negative editorials about Haile Selassie and his policies, accusing him of failing to identify himself with fellow Black people and of being visionless and disloyal to his country. He criticised Selassie for leaving Ethiopia and seeking exile in Bath, England (1936-1940) when his country came under attack from Italian forces. During the same year, he organized the School of African Philosophy, which would train the future leaders of the U.N.I.A.

In 1940, five years after his arrival in London, Garvey fell ill; he suffered a stroke in January, which left him partially paralyzed. While his health slowly improved under special care, his doctors diagnosed that two previous bouts of pneumonia had left him with a weak heart. In May 1940, a London reporter sent out a news release that Garvey had died and newspapers all over the world carried the news. Daisy White, Garvey's personal secretary stated that as he opened all his letters and cables, "he was faced with clippings of his own obituary and pictures of himself with deep Black borders. After the second day of this pile of shock, he collapsed in his chair and could hardly be understood after that". Marcus Garvey steadily grew worse and passed away on 10 June 1940, having never set foot in Africa.

Marcus Garvey was buried in St Mary's Roman Catholic Cemetery in Kensal Green, London. However, on 13 November 1964 the remains of the Right Excellent Marcus Mosiah Garvey were exhumed and returned to National Heroes Park, Kingston, Jamaica. It was here that Garvey was declared Jamaica's first national hero.

Garvey had contended that Black people should not only work for self-improvement, but be economically self-reliant and politically self-determinant. He argued and preached against the ravages of racism and espoused the pride of being Black. He was particularly vociferous against 'Mulattoes', who he argued had one foot in the Black world and the other in the White one. He denounced Du Bois as a Mulatto, and ridiculed those who would pass themselves off as White. Garvey claimed that Black people of African descent should have the option to be repatriated back to Africa.

In attempting to break the curse of slavery, these three stalwarts used their influence, connections and skills to galvanise the Black community. However, the affects of the Trans-Atlantic slave trade on Black communities throughout the world has been so pervasive that their numerous efforts were scuppered. This has serious implications for those who are part of the Christian church and have not been delivered from this mindset.

Chapter 4
THEOLOGICAL ACTIVISM

The term 'Theology' is a construct of two Greek words: 'Theos' and 'Logos'. Theos is translated as 'God' and Logos as 'word'. Therefore, the literal translation would be 'God's word' or 'the word about God'. Theology is that study of the word of God and it follows then that there can be many theologies, which are determined by the location, the experiences and the culture of those developing them. Simply put, theology is 'God talk'. This section of the book is interested in how Black people talk about and relate to God. It is particularly interested in how former enslaved Africans mediated their faith in the face of colonialism and oppression. I will also examine the forms of theological activism used to conscientise the Black community and the development of 'Black theology' in Britain and the USA.

Survival

In the face of virulent, rampant racism, the former slave community not only embraced the God of the Christian Bible, they also started to look to him to deliver them from the shackles of the past. The Exodus narrative tells of a benevolent God who saw their plight, heard their cries and came down to deliver them. With basic education now being afforded to the masses, they started to dream. However, the dreams were about a life free from troubles and legacies of slavery that they were living through. Some commentators insist that the hymnology and the 'Negro spiritual' songs were a means of maintaining their sanity and giving them hope for the future. Some songs, such as 'swing low sweet chariot', which is used as an anthem by the current English national rugby team, were used to convey messages to those who planned to escape from their enslavement.

After three hundred years in enslavement, many from the Black community attempted to reconnect with their past. Influenced by the Maroons and the Haitians, several religio-political groups sprang up, their mandate was to physically return to Africa or create a milieu where they were spiritually connected to their ancestors. However, they faced difficulties caused by location and identification.

Identity

The argument around the legacy of slavery on the Caribbean Diaspora and on African people in general, is a hotly contested one and is crystallised via the Melville Herskovits versus E. Franklin Frazier debate. On the one hand, E. Franklin Frazer posited that African-American and African Caribbean culture developed as an imitation of European culture. He argued that the experience of slavery had been so devastating that it completely stripped enslaved Africans of all aspects of their own culture. Conversely, Melville Herskovits provided evidence from research in anthropology, folklore and history to support his argument for the continuity of various aspects of African culture in the Americas and Caribbean. It can be argued that there is good evidence to support Herskovits' contention, particularly when an analysis is made of the spirituality of African American and African Caribbean people. Although there are aspects of European culture and practices that are 'embedded' in the culture of the African Diaspora community, many of the traits learned over generations in Africa remain today.

Academics point to the fact that a significant part of being human is our ability to remember. Being fully human is to have an autobiographical self and not be trapped in the present or the past, but being able to draw on experiences in myriad ways. The American neuroscientist, Antonio Damasio, author of *The feeling of what happens,* has examined many Americans with impaired brain function and as a result has learnt much about the circuitry that gives rise to normal waking consciousness, and an autobiographical sense of self. He states that intrinsically, memory is studied at different levels, from the molecular changes in synapses and neurons in the brain, to the various types of cognitive processing of stored information and the emotional dynamics of remembering. There are a number of differing models of memory, but in broad terms, memory comes in two forms: short-term memory and long-term memory. Short-term memory or "active memory" is the capacity for holding a small amount of information in mind in an active, readily available state for a short period. Without rehearsal or active maintenance, the duration of short-term memory is believed to be in the order of seconds. In contrast, long-term memory indefinitely stores a seemingly unlimited amount of information. Long-term memory is sub-divided into several categories, such as procedural memory, where we remember how to ride a bike, brush our teeth etc. The variety of remembering that we do, short-term and long-term, relies on lots of different neural circuitry and storage sites, all of which stack up together to make us fully human in our remembering, in our consciousness, in our self-awareness and in our identity. Without remembering, we are deprived of the essentials of being human.

How we capture, define and retain life's events are divided and sub-divided in other aspects of memory. All the various aspects of remembering give us an indelible link and continuity with the past. This continuity carries affects that are difficult to delete, even with skilled psycho-therapy. And in terms of this life, these memories are forever. Melville Herskovit's thesis proves this.

Similarly, a study by Joy DeGruy-Leary in 2005 highlights the traumas of slavery and the psychological effects they still have on the descendants of those who were enslaved nearly two hundred years after abolition in the USA. Dr DeGruy-Leary highlights the affect that Post-Traumatic Stress Disorder (PTSD) has on victims of vicious rape, victims of serious accidents, victims of natural disasters and so on. And since enslaved Africans were subjected to many dehumanising and oppressive occurrences, she argues that they and their descendants suffer from Post-Traumatic Slave Syndrome (PTSS), which is similar to symptoms suffered by the Holocaust victims. She argues that the result of this is the rage and frustration handed down to descendants of enslaved Africans, and she concludes that other visible effects include the feelings of low self-esteem and a sense of worthlessness that are still prevalent among many African Americans. This psychological condition can only be healed when the victims are allowed to tell their stories and are encouraged to locate themselves in their history, and so break the cycle of oppression and recapture positive images of African people prior to enslavement. Liberation and transformation occur by locating the individual in their context so that they are able to connect with their past.

Since the vast majority of people from the Caribbean Diaspora community are of the Christian faith, it is paramount to look at how the memory was captured in the

Judeo-Christian narrative of the enslaved Hebrews of the Bible to show the importance of continuity with the past. It is from the Exodus narrative in the Bible that the enslaved communities learned about a God who liberates people who are enslaved.

The use of symbols and icons

The slave masters Christianised a vast majority of the enslaved community in the Caribbean and America. As a means of discontinuity, they were given 'Christian' names. This process of having two names, a 'dressing' and a 'judging' name is still prevalent in the Caribbean, particularly Jamaica. Members of the enslaved community, as do many oppressed people, read or heard the Jewish sacred texts and extrapolated the notion that the God of the Bible would liberate the oppressed from the clutches of a Suzerain oppressor. There seems to be an existential link between the plight of the African-Caribbean enslaved community and their descendants and Israelite slave community in Egypt. It must be noted that the Bible is contextual and that the Exodus narrative is read and re-read by liberationists who appropriate it for their context. It is also apparent that in re-reading this text, the reader is re-interpreting and adding their slant to it. In addition, some will accept these texts as fact and therefore history, while others will see them as folklore and myths. Alistair Kee has suggested that although Latin American and African-American theologians use these texts and presupposes that God frees slaves; he does not free slaves but uses the Hebrews in Egypt to fulfil His purposes. This perspective is the typical White andocentric viewpoint.

I want to examine the Hebrew community in slavery in Egypt and explain how they kept their continuity with the past by maintaining their rites and rituals to demonstrate that, even in situations of complete powerlessness, there is continuity with the past that is difficult to eradicate – akin to an individual's memory of the past. This is one main reason that so many practices such as Obeah, Juju, Santeria and other traditional African practices found their way into the theology of the African Caribbean Christian community.

When we consider the Israelite community of the Exodus and the trauma they experienced in Egypt, we notice that they had physical and ceremonial rites to connect them with their past and maintain their identity. It is obvious that Old Testament faith was not cognitive and detached but was participative and holistic. The enslaved community had 'signs' or rituals such as the 'rainbow', Genesis 9:13 and 'circumcision' Genesis 17, to remember the covenant made with Yahweh. All these events had theological significance. Some were icons and communal, while others were personal and familial. Nonetheless, they were a means by which the community remembered those events of the past and made links with them. Today in North London, there are still Jewish communities who wear the blue tassel mentioned in Numbers 15:39 as a public mark of communal identity and of continuity with the past. Also feasts instituted over 3,000 years ago are still celebrated by both the Jewish and the Christian communities today.

Unlike their Jewish counterparts, African Americans were actively encouraged to jettison everything African and to become a new hybrid community. Some scholars argue that the discontinuity was not as great as it is made out to be, and that the new community rethought their social and cultural context, thus creating new means of remembering and dealing with the past. This new community spent the majority of its time finding ways and means to survive post emancipation. Essentially the descendants of enslaved Africans were encouraged to view the European God through the lens of the White slave master and to be a benevolent servant whilst serving him. Liberation and fulfilment would only be achieved in the after-life. This mindset became the norm for a vast majority 'who bought into' the sin of racism and the pigmentocratic regime implemented by the colonialists.

The slaves used their memory of stories and rituals passed to them from previous generations to maintain continuity with the past and hence to maintain their humanity. Hence, today we have 'Ananci' stories, melodies from West African laments and African proverbs maintained across the Caribbean Diaspora. These are some of the symbols used by the descendants of enslaved Africans to reconnect with the past.

Re-thinking theology

The quest for an identity that connected with the past and gave the individual dignity was now the major task of the conscientised community. The three stalwarts mentioned earlier sought for ways to change the lot of the Black community via various means. Booker T. Washington sought to do this through hard work; Du Bois through education and social action and Marcus Garvey used by a combination of both, but also encouraged Black people to think highly of themselves and of Africa.

Many independent Black churches emerged after manumission because of the racist systems that existed in the Americas and across Europe, Black clergy and academics looked for a methodology of describing the God of the Judeo-Christian scriptures who was not made in the image of their former slave masters. Most forms of liberation theology were born in the social turmoil of the 1960s and these new thinkers were not concerned with the intellectual challenge posed by atheism and secularism, but the social, economic and political oppression experienced by people in the present day. For liberation thinkers, theology needed to shift its focus from abstract speculation on the nature and existence of God to the concrete realities of how the gospel might serve to reverse the oppressive and burdensome conditions in which so many people languished, particularly Black people. They held that God was reconceived as the One who was pre-eminently involved in and virtually identified with the struggle for liberation. The older theological emphasis on divine *transcendence*, in which God is viewed as distinct from and sovereign over the world, gradually gave way to divine *immanence* in which God is known and seen only as far as he is active in setting free the oppressed.

And so Black theology was born in the 1960s with the view of bringing liberation to a significant portion of God's creation, the Black person.

What is Black theology?

All theology is contextual, that is to say, it is inextricably linked to and thus shaped by the unique social and cultural factors in which it is forged. Theology is not formulated "from above", detached from the concrete historical dynamics of life on earth. It is the expression "from below" out of a specific cultural milieu and thus reflects the unique needs and aspirations of the people who articulate it. Liberation theologians "seek a truly indigenous [Latin American] theology that arises out of an involvement in its unique socio-political realities" (Grenz/Olson, 215). Since theology is contextual language for a particular time and place, the scholars write as informed by their cultural perspective. The sources and norms of theology are the formative factors that determine the character of a given theology. The norm of a particular theology is the hermeneutical principles used to evaluate its sources. Hermeneutics is the interpreting of scripture in its context. Therefore, the norm of Black theology is the manifestation of Jesus as the Black Christ, who provides the vehicle for Black liberation.

Black theology or 'Black God talk' uses experience as one of its leading major tenets. This is opposite to Liberal and Progressive Liberal theologies, which use conversation, interpretation and understanding as their foremost tools. A major task of Black theology is to identify how God's liberating acts will become evident through experience in the communities where it is operating. In Britain, Black theology is far different from that arising in America. Like liberation theology arising from poverty in South America, Black theology arose out of the struggles of the civil right movement as articulated by James Cone *et al*, and was concerned with the church's response to civil rights during the sixties. On the contrary, the development and articulation of Black theology in the UK, is predominantly by descendants from the African-Caribbean Diaspora community.

Therefore, Black theology is defined as the experience of God as articulated by the very people who have experienced racism, marginalisation and oppression and have not been able to tell their own stories until now. I am aware of the anti-essentialists Black theologians, who view the problems facing people from the African Diaspora as poverty, economics and structural power, and therefore move away from the modernist, neo-colonialist perspective, which starts with a critique of racism as its foundation. They argue that the proponents of Black theology are still rooted to and are defined by modernist dichotomies such as race and class.

James Cone was one of the chief architects of Black theology. As part of his theological analysis, Cone argues for God's identification with "blackness", and that, "The Black theologian must reject any conception of God which stifles Black self-determination by picturing God as a God of all peoples. Either God is identified with the oppressed to the point that their experience becomes God's experience, or God is a God of racism. The Blackness of God means that God has made the oppressed condition his own condition. This is the essence of the biblical revelation. By electing Israelite slaves as 'the people of God' and by becoming the Oppressed One in Jesus Christ, the human race is made to understand that God is known where human beings experience humiliation and suffering. Liberation is not an afterthought, but the very essence of divine activity. (*A Black Theology of Liberation*, pp. 63-64, 1970)

Nascent Black theology was a polemic against racism and Eurocentric liberal theology for its lack of commentary on institutionalised racism. Black churchmen and theologians, many of whom were educated in these White denominational church seminaries, were convinced that the God of scripture was not a racist and hence was concerned about the marginalisation and oppression of a large majority of his creation. In 1967 at the National Conference of Black Churchmen, in Washington D.C., these radical Black clergy split from their White counterparts in the National Council of Churches and formed a Black Caucus, which would report on the urban crisis in society at the time. They issued a statement, which in their minds was their opportunity to reclaim the true meaning of the gospel that was to respond to the needs of a downtrodden, alienated people. They said: "We confess that in recent times we have not lived up to our heritage, for we have not celebrated, preserved and enhanced the integrity of Blackness. Rather, we have fallen prey to the dominance of white society and have allowed the truth, meaningfulness and authenticity of the Black church to be defamed by our easy acceptance of its goals, objectives and criteria for success.   Therefore, the Black church has unwittingly become a tool for our oppression, providing an easy vehicle for escape from the harsh realities of our own existence. This of necessity makes it impossible for us to be instruments of liberation which is our calling as Christians and particularly Black Christians." *For My People*, p.16, James Cone, 1984.

These churchmen openly embraced the Black Power movement and saw it as an occasion for fighting the demonic presence of racism in the White church, and as an opportunity to reclaim their true mission of liberation. Black theology as a term to describe the theology of the Black churchmen and theologians, emerged from the formation of the National Conference of Black Churchmen (NCBC) in 1967. However, the actual term 'Black theology' is attributed to Grant S. Shockley, a Black Christian educator, who used it in an article entitled, "Ultimatum and Hope" in Christian Century, 12 February 1969.   Therefore, Black theology as articulated by the NCBC was an interpretation of the faith of Black people in the light of Black history and culture, which is completely separate from 'White religion'.

How did the civil rights movement influence the development of Black theology?

The Three contexts for the development of Black Theology
As the civil rights movement of the 1960s gained momentum under the leadership of Martin Luther King Jr and others, Black churchmen began to relate the Christian gospel to the struggle for racial justice in America. This movement for social justice galvanised the Black community

but drove a wedge between Black churchmen and their White counterparts, who insisted that politics and religion did not mix. Therefore, from their perspective, boycotts, sit-ins and freedom marches were inconsequential. This movement led many Black theologians to see this fight for social justice as a continuation of the fight for freedom from slavery and to reaffirm that, the God of the Christian scriptures did not create slaves or second-class citizens. With this in mind, Black preachers and theologians of the time, rejected racism and affirmed the Black struggle for liberation as consistent with the gospel of Jesus. This initiated the development of Black theology.

Another major influence in the development of Black theology was that of a book entitled *Black Religion,* written by Joseph Washington. In it he argued that, since Black culture was unique, there must be a uniquely Black religion that was different from White religion and that would exist alongside established religions such as Protestantism, Catholicism and so on. He further argued that since Black people were excluded from White churches, their religion or form of Christianity was not genuine. Therefore, Black people only had 'folk religion' and 'folk theology'. To refute Washington's argument, Black theologians and the Black churchmen of the NCBC wrote to correct two misconception that he had proposed, namely, 'Black religion' is not Christian religion and that the 'Christian gospel' had nothing to do with the struggle for justice. Therefore, in contending that it was 'Black religion' which was truly Christian and that, the gospel identified with the struggle for justice, they developed a Black theology of liberation. This was opposite to White theology and to the White churches that preached about love but ignored justice and also preached about equality but practised racial segregation.

The final major influence was the statement of a group of radical churchmen from the National Committee of Negro Churchmen, who refused to denounce Black Power as un-Christian. They published a 'Black Power Statement' in the New York Times on 31 July 1966 which argued that White theology and the Christianity that justified it, was bankrupt, since they either supported or were silent on racism, and that Black Christians needed to construct their own

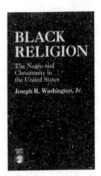

interpretation of the scriptures and connect it with their African heritage. It is from this viewpoint that James Cone and Gayraud Wilmore later developed their thinking about Black theology in an attempt to develop a constructive and systematic process for describing Black faith.

It is out of the crisis in the urban cities of America, that Black theology emerged, as a means of describing and articulating the Christian faith, in response to the Black power movement. Black scholars like Gayraud Wilmore, James Cone, Preston Williams, J. Deotis Roberts and those from all strands of the Christian spectrum, began to reflect on the nature of Blackness in relation to Black Power, Black history, and the Black church etc.

James Cone's first reflection on the subject was entitled *Black theology and Black Power which* he wrote to demonstrate that Black Power was the political wing of Black theology, although the proponents of the Black Power movement were definitely anti-Christian and saw Christianity as the White man's religion. To solve this dichotomy, Cone and his contemporaries developed Black theology as a means of making Christianity relevant. This had the affect of combining Christianity and Blackness by holding in tension the need for the liberation that the gospel of Jesus should bring and the need for political activism that was characterised by the Black Power movement.

Black theology in the UK

The influx of African-Caribbean migrants to the UK in the late 1950s and early 1960s radically changed the church going population in Britain. The arrival of the 492 Caribbean people on the SS Empire Windrush in June 1948 seemed to belie the fact that Black people had been present in Britain since the time of the Roman invasion; indeed, there was a large presence of up to 20,000 living in London in the late 1700's. [Ian Duffield, "Blacks in Britain: History and the Historians", History Today (Vol.31, Sept. 1981), p.34.].

However, these migrants came to these shores from across the British colonies at the request of the then Labour Government (1945-1951), to help to rebuild the country after World War II. Since the colonial population were all British citizens, many saw it as their duty to come to the aid of the Mother Country. The influx of migrants reached its peak in 1961 when more than 74,000 Caribbean people entered the UK. To stem the tide of Caribbean migrants, the Conservative Government (1957-1963) passed the

Commonwealth Immigration Act in 1962, whose remit was to limit the Black presence in the UK. This migrant population came to Britain having been convinced that the streets were paved with gold and that over a five year period they would have made their fortunes to return to their respective Islands and live in a big house. Their expectations were dashed when they arrived in the UK; not only were they confronted with disdain, overt racism and signs over rooms for rent declaring: - "no Black, dogs or Irish", the gold on the streets turned out to be dog muck.

The vast majority of these migrants were practising Christians from a wide variety of the established churches. Many were members of Pentecostal churches with their headquarters in the United States, where the leadership and congregations were invariably White. Bishop Joe Aldred argues that many of the migrants came as missionaries, but on arrival in the UK they faced racism and were ostracised from their traditional denominations. This in part led to the numerous 'Black-led' churches that are present today. The term 'Black-led', which became a contentious one among Black Christians, was popularised by the German academic, Roswith Gerloff, in a piece of research carried out in the early 1970s.

The writer and theologian Mark Sturge gives a detailed reflection on the different strands of Black churches in Britain, their distinctive theology and praxis, and uses the term Black Majority Church (BMC). However, Sturge only focuses on BMC's from the Pentecostal traditions and does not explore those in the historic denominations, which make up two thirds of the Black Christian presence in Britain. Also, Sturge, acting as an insider looking out, lists and categorises the Black presence in Britain and does not critique their praxis through the lens of Black theological principles. Nor does he suggest a framework for liberation and transformation.

It is important to recognise that there is a distinction between Black Christian religious experience and Black theology. Black Christian religious experience can be defined as 'the approach to Christian traditions that arise out of Black experiences but which do not have a political or transformative agenda. For Black Christian religious experience, 'Blackness' is not the primary hermeneutical tool for interpreting the Christian faith, nor is Black experience given pole position, although the dividing line between Black Christian religious experience and Black theology is somewhat blurred.' On the other hand, Black theology is the discipline of interpreting Christian traditions and practices by using the Black experiences as the primary hermeneutical lens through which the truth of God's liberating agency is discerned and displayed.

The roots of Black theology in the UK

The formation of these multifaceted denominations, particularly from the Pentecostal stream, did not lead to much theological reflection. And as Paulo Friere states in his classic book, *Pedagogy of the oppressed*, 'Action without reflection is mere activism, and reflection without action is mere verbalism.' Many of the leaders of these new churches were not only bi-vocational they had little or no formal theological training. Therefore, there was a vast amount of verbalism and very little activism from the pulpit, and as stated by Robert Beckford, 'these leaders were terrified of discussing anything political in their sermons'. In an essay in *Post Colonial Black Theology*, 2007, Beresford Lewis vigorously refutes this point. He argues for the themes of celebration, dialogue and critical and constructive engagement to bridge the gap between the pulpit, the pew and the academy for BMC's. As stated earlier, the majority of Black Christians were located in the traditional denominations, and it is from within these denominations that Black ministers started to articulate and reflect on the issues facing the migrant population.

Although many of these Black Pentecostal churches were attracting large amounts of the migrant population, their focus was on the 'salvation of the soul', having the 'right dress code' and making preparation for heaven. Unlike their counterparts in America, there was little or no concern about social justice issues or active engagement with the political process although the vast majority of their congregants voted for the left-of-centre Labour Party. Black Christians went to church, worked hard and allowed the natural order to progress. There was virtually no engagement with the work of Black theologians or Black theology in the United States, although the larger denominations such as the New Testament Church of God, the Church of God of Prophecy and the United Pentecostal Church all had their headquarters in the USA.

The development of Black theology in the UK arises from the reflections of Black scholars who have published works challenging the sin of racism in society and in the Christian church in particular. The first such work to be published was a text titled, *The New Black Presence,* written in 1976 by Gus John. In this British Council of Churches sponsored work, John outlines the challenges that Britain in general, and the church in particular, would face with the arrival of the post-colonial migrants. Although John highlighted the numerous challenges that the ecclesiastical church or the body of Christ would face, he did not confront White Christianity concerning their liturgy and praxis. Four years after Gus John's article, the Revd Robinson Milwood, a

Methodist minister serving in north London, made this challenge. Although Milwood did not expressively call himself a Black liberation theologian, nor was his text an expression of Black theology in Britain, his work articulated the themes and motifs on which Black theology is predicated, such as challenging the structures within White Christianity. For Milwood, these structures were erected to propagate White hegemony, while simultaneously dismissing the cultures and experiences of Black Christians in their churches. Milwood wanted to effect reconciliation between Black and White Christians, and for the predominantly White majority church to recognise and accept the cultures and identities of Black and minority ethnic Christians. After writing *Let's Get together*, his tone changed and in his next work, *Salvation as Liberation,* he radically challenged White liberals and their racist attitude towards Black people in Britain. In his *Liberation and Mission* one can see the emergence of a nascent Black British theology that challenges racism, argues for social justice and critiques the lack analysis of racism in theological institutes throughout the UK.

White clergy and scholars were also instrumental in the development of Black theology in Britain. Roswith Gerloff's work was the first academic attempt to identify a Black British theology in post World War II Britain. She worked for a Para church organisation called the 'Centre for Black and White Christian Partnership' in Birmingham and coined the term 'black-led'. The growing movement of mainly independent Pentecostal Churches in Britain fuelled Gerloff's research and was one of the first pieces of academic work to try to identify a distinct Black British Theology (1991). However, her work failed in its attempt to identify a 'Black British Theology'; what she identified was the variety of Black Christian expressions in Britain, many of whom had little knowledge or inclination of liberating or transforming their communities. Gerloff, as an outsider looking in, made the cardinal error of assuming that the Black Christian experience was the same as Black theology and that the majority of Black Christians worshipped in these Black churches. Evidence shows that the Black Christian religious experience has no distinct mandate for liberation, social justice or political activism.

The Revd John Wilkinson, a White Anglican minister from Birmingham was also instrumental in the development of Black theology in Britain. Wilkinson started the first Black Christian Studies programme in Britain, and was one of the first people to write an academic piece of work about the Black presence in White majority churches. Wilkinson was a pioneer in the development of Black theology in Britain and paved the way for Robert Beckford, one of Britain's most celebrated Black theologians.

As the level of conscientisation rose among the Diaspora community during the 1980s, Black British ministers, sociologists and theologians began to engage with Black theologians in the USA, and started to articulate a political rather than racial use of the term 'Black' as an umbrella under which all marginalised, racialised or oppressed groups could coalesce. Books such as *A Time to Speak* and its sequel *A Time to Act* (edited by Raj Patel and Paul Grant); *Jesus is Dread* and *Dread and Pentecostal* by Robert Beckford and the inception of a journal entitled *Black Theology in Britain: A Journal of Contextual Praxis* edited by a Ghanaian, Revd Dr Emmanuel Lartey, firmly established a British Black theology whose roots were firmly established in the academy.

Although Black theology was established in Britain, it was not a discipline with which Black Majority Churches engaged. Therefore, those people who were instrumental in its conception had little input into these churches and the churches themselves were suspicious of those who were members of the academy. Robert Beckford attempted to bridge this gap by articulating a political theology for the Pentecostal churches by using the polemic term, 'Dread' as a motif for articulating and doing theology. His attempt to mobilise the Pentecostal churches to move from a literal reading of the biblical text to re-reading the text through the lens of Black British theology never took off. Sadly, more White church congregations use Beckford's material than do the Black church leaders for whom he wrote it.

The virtues of Black theology

Black theology by its very name will have the affect of locating young Black people in their context. It will give them a sense of identity, connectivity and continuity with the past. Black theology will also make young Black people aware of the pervasive nature of racism and how deeply embedded it is in the British culture. This means that they have to be twice as good to get half as far as their White counterparts. And finally they will be conscientised to the fact that God, as revealed in Jesus Christ, is on their side, since the biblical narrative repeatedly tells us that Jesus has come to set the captives free and liberate those who are oppressed and marginalised (Luke 4:18ff, Isaiah 61:1-3.).

The Problems with Black theology

This discipline focuses on experience as its starting point. Therefore, in attempting to re-read the biblical narrative through the lens of Black experience the essence of the gospel can be lost. The good news of the gospel, as articulated in the Christian scriptures, states that God, as incarnated as Jesus Christ, came to liberate all people from their sin for the sole purpose of reconciling them back to himself (Isaiah 9:1-7; 61:1-4; Matthew 1:18-25; 2 Corinthians 5:16-21). By starting with experience, Black theology runs the risks of becoming just another pressure group seeking to right the wrongs of the last 400 years.

Also, Black theology started life as an academic reflection on the dichotomy of Black people being told that they were part of the body of Christ, when in reality they lived in the poorest ghettos and had the worst educational chances. This meant that they were employed in menial jobs and were discriminated against in the various denominations that they belonged to. Although Black theologians reflected on these contradictions, it had no practical answers to them, since in essence Black theology was an academic tool.

Finally, Black theology started out as a polemic against racism and it is still emerging. By engaging with other expressions where Blackness is the primary hermeneutical lens, such as Black theology from South Africa, Womanist theology and Black Christian education of liberation, it can be grouped with movements such as the Gay Christian lobby, the Feminist movement and far right Christian movements, which skews how Black people are represented.

Chapter 5
SOCIAL TRANSFORMATION

The need for an educational system which incorporates Blackness as its central concept arises from the development of racism in ancient and modern society, and in the history of the Christian church. Racism is usually defined as views, practices and actions reflecting the belief that humanity is divided into distinct biological groups called 'races', and that members of a certain race share particular attributes which make that group as a whole less desirable, more desirable, inferior or superior.

The exact definition of racism is controversial because scholars disagree about the meaning of the concept 'race', also there is little agreement about what constitutes discrimination. Critics argue that the term is applied differentially, with a focus on such prejudices by Whites, defining mere observations of racial differences as racism. Some definitions would have it that any assumption that a person's behaviour would be influenced by their racial categorisation is racist, regardless of whether the action is intentionally harmful or pejorative. Other definitions only include consciously malignant forms of discrimination. Among the questions about how to define racism, are the questions of whether to include forms of discrimination that are unintentional. This includes making assumptions about preferences or the abilities of others based on racial stereotypes, whether to include symbolic or institutionalized forms of discrimination, such as the circulation of ethnic stereotypes through the media, and whether to include the socio-political dynamics of social stratification that sometimes have a racial component. Some definitions of racism also include discriminatory behaviours and beliefs based on cultural, national, ethnic, caste, or religious stereotypes. According to the United Nations' convention, there is no distinction between the terms racial discrimination and ethnic discrimination and superiority based on racial differentiation is scientifically false, morally condemnable, socially unjust and dangerous and that there is no justification for racial discrimination, in theory or in practice, anywhere.

There is little doubt that transformation only occurs when people are educated. And the definition of 'educate' is to draw out. When the Caribbean people came to the Promised Land of Britain in the 1940s, 50s and 60s, they were unaware that the British education system would discriminate against their children. Since the early 1970s, several community activists have highlighted the problem of underachievement among Black children in the British education system.

Miss-education

Bernard Coard, a Grenadian teacher brought the problems facing the Black community into stark reality in the early 1970s with the publication "How the West Indian Child is made Educationally Subnormal in the British School System". Coard's book highlighted the deliberate ploy of British educators to deny the children of the migrant Black population a decent education. Coard proved that the educational progress of African-Caribbean children in their charge was definitely subdued. In his book, he cites three reasons why African-Caribbean children, and boys in particular, were failing in the British education system such as:

- low expectation by the pupils due to curricula, identity and other issues
- low motivation to succeed academically
- low expectation on the part of teachers, which affected the amount of effort expended on pupils.

Other Black professionals realised that the authorities were not addressing the educational issues, but were trying to address the problem from a socio-psychological perspective, with the main aim of raising the negative self-image and self-concept of the Black child which was an integral part of their system. In her book, 'Educating the Black Child', Maureen Stone argued that this obscured the real issues of racial oppression and powerlessness. As one who had successfully navigated the schools in Britain, Dr Tony Sewell called for more Afro-centric images and tools to be incorporated in the education of Black children in the UK.

Patterns of behaviour analogous to those of the rebellious enslaved African people in the early nineteenth century are now commonplace in Britain, as young people failed by the education system are falling foul of the criminal justice system. The real argument is whether Christian education is the answer, and if so, how can it become part of the national education system.

There is clear evidence to show that the Christian gospel has the ability to set all captives free. This freedom is dependent on how the gospel is contextualised and its delivery. This leads to the question of whether Christian education or Christian education of liberation is relevant to the marginalised, the oppressed or those living under a curse?

What is Black Christian education?

Christian education can mean different things to different people. However, most scholars would understand the phrase as it applies to the process of Christian formation or to the intellectual development of a critical evaluation of the Christian faith. Others restrict it to a particular way of learning Christianity, while others still use the term to denote a critique of general education or the philosophy of education from a Christian perspective, [see Jeff Astley, *The Contours of Christian Education*]. For the purposes of this book, Black Christian education is defined as education done by Black people with a Christian ethos for the purpose of nurturing and transforming young people.

There are certain aspects of Black Christian education which are paramount such as Christian education being prophetic, that is, it must be relevant now, but also have a future impact and must reflect the world-view from which it speaks. It must also be liberating as it expresses God's concern for the oppressed. Lastly, it must reflect the cultural, social and historical experiences and expressions of the faith of African Caribbean peoples and those with an African phenotype in which that faith it is practised. In the USA, Grant Shockley, an African-American educationalist, defined Black Christian education within the Black church as 'the process that teaches concepts, attitudes and skills which facilitate meaningful learning in relation to the Black experience'.

Since one of the aims of Christian education is to make the gospel relevant to people so that they can meaningfully understand it and apply it to their daily lives, one is faced with the real question of how to get the process out of the faith domain and into general education. More importantly, how can it be honed so that it can transform and nurture disenfranchised young adolescents? The idea of faith as an integral part of the education process is a contentious one among some educators. Indeed, some secular humanists will argue that faith has no place in the educative process. Notwithstanding these views, Thomas Groome, a Roman Catholic educator, and others from the faith domain, are adamant that faith is instrumental in the successful learning and teaching process. Faith is also an integral part of the history of the African-Caribbean Diaspora community in Britain, and is indelibly linked with their education. However, a major hurdle in overcoming social exclusion and bringing about social transformation is that of identity. Studies show that when you are able to connect with your past you can define and locate your identity.

Who am I?

The difficulty for the African Diaspora community is to determine exactly where their identity is located. From an anthropological viewpoint, the African Caribbean community has looked in many places to determine its location. Young African Caribbean people and many Africans from the Diaspora sought identity in a plethora of Afro-centric movements, such as Rastafari, the Nation of Islam, the Back to Africa and the Ausar Auset movements. For young Black boys it is in gangs or crews. This has led to the dialectic struggle for reality, which W.E.B Du Bois called 'double consciousness'.

When the second-generation of African Caribbean people became an integral part of British society in the early 1980s, race and identity became a huge problem for many African Caribbean and mixed heritage young people. Racism, poor housing and low career possibilities exacerbated the situation for many. Margaret Thatcher, the then leader of the

Conservative Government, was instrumental in shifting racism from socio-biology to culture. Now the ex-colonial subjects, whose fore-parents were grossly abused and vilified on the Caribbean plantations, were living next door to their former masters. These adolescents, particularly the young males, were seeking meanings to what it meant to be Black.

Not all Black scholars are convinced about the notions of authentic Blackness; Victor Anderson the author of '*Beyond Ontological Blackness*' is one such academic. While Cornell West states that Blackness is a form of moral reasoning within a prophetic framework where morals and ethics are 'lived out' equitably. Therefore, since Blackness is defined here as a political term, the phenotype that determines how people are seen, that is, the fact that people are descended from Africa, may become irrelevant when it comes to defining them as Black. Dwight Hopkins states that Blackness is far more than a political and ethical construct and should not be confined to a phenotypical state, since the identity of an individual involves their culture, world-view, spirituality and many other aspects. According to the academic Les Back, young people in Britain have turned to music and have formed a hybrid identity, which is now Black youth culture. This is where the majority of young African Caribbean people are located now. Therefore, to effect change it is necessary to engage with the culture and work to transform the negative elements of that culture.

Social transformation can only occur when all the citizens have similar opportunities to be educated are conscientised. The gospel must give the individual tools so that they can be economically independent, socially active and spiritually free. Finding one's cultural location is one aspect of a many faceted coin. Black young individuals need to learn about the history, culture and the achievements of their ancestors, and need the social and spiritual tools to rid themselves of the

75

inherited mental shackles and the unhealed scars that still surface due to the ravages of the enslavement of their ancestors.

It is in the pages of the Holy Bible that we find the wisdom of God, which is available to everyone who dares to make Jesus his or her Lord. It is because of his atoning sacrifice that the impossible becomes possible and those who were marginalised, abused and denigrated because of their skin colour, can once again become kings, priests and presidents of nations.

Chapter 6

THE BIBLICAL NOTION OF IDENTITY IN THE FINISHED WORK OF CHRIST

There is little doubt that Black churches can lead the way in reversing the ravages of chattel enslavement and educate Black youth in Britain. This can be achieved via the application of the tenets of Black theology highlighted in the previous chapter, namely, connectivity with the past, knowledge of who they are and to whom they belong. However, prior to this, the individuals need be liberated culturally and historically to know themselves.

The biblical narrative in Romans 12 encourages Christians to 'be transformed' psychologically and spiritually 'by the renewing of [their] minds'. This renewal will counteract and quash the myth that an individual who is Black or from the Diaspora cannot achieve emotionally, spiritually and physically. Since our minds are the 'battle ground' where the war rages, our enemy uses negative thoughts, suggestions and inference to get us to believe a lie. We must actively challenge the psychological impact of racist theories and methodologies that state that Black folks are only capable of excelling at physical work. This must be challenged vehemently. Likewise, any negativity that underpins low self-esteem, harmful self-images and the propensity to buy into the media representation of Black people should be boldly challenged. On the other hand,

Black people must not become so Black focussed that they start to hate everything that is not Black; we must love our neighbours as we love ourselves.

The very first step is to love ourselves; love who you are and what God has ordained for you to become. In essence, the battle of the mind starts with the individual having a positive self-image, which jettisons and moves beyond double consciousness and White hegemony. Reading copiously about our heritage allows the minds to be renewed and when this is underpinned with the word of God, the individual is on their way towards healing, deliverance and total restoration. By doing this the individual will then be transformed into the image and likeness of Jesus. This does not mean becoming a Jew or Caucasian, but becoming a person of integrity, character and spiritual awareness.

For many from the Caribbean Diaspora this is not a problem, as the default belief system incorporates God at all levels. Indeed, it is from African traditional folk religion, imported to the Caribbean, that many beliefs and practices find their way into Africanised Christianity. And so we have in the Caribbean a vast amount of syncretism or re-interpretation of the gospels for that context, so much so that the culture of the vast majority of Christians from the Caribbean is to go to church on Sunday, but also to hold on to a large amount of traditional beliefs. Some African-Caribbean folk religions emphasize magical practices designed to bring good luck to their devotees or harm to their enemies, and include ceremonies that often involve the ritual sacrifice of animals. These religions worship the spirits of the dead, which is anti-Christ. Furthermore, the spirits are given the names of Christian saints so that this blending of beliefs allowed enslaved Africans to retain their native faith while appearing to convert to Christianity.

Consequently, there are many in the Caribbean who professes to be Christians, but feel comfortable with the rituals of these folk religions. In some ways, this is similar to the Christianisation of many pagan festivals by the Church Fathers who, for instance, chose the date used by the Druids to celebrate the Winter Solstice as the time to celebrate the birth of Jesus. And the Feast of Easter when pagans celebrated the goddess of fertility, Astarte, to celebrate the death, burial and resurrection of our Lord Jesus. The Fathers were rejecting everything Jewish except Jesus.

When In 1998 Pope John Paul II visited Cuba, he urged Catholics there to reject the practice of Santeria, which is practised widely across the Caribbean and is known by different names. In Jamaica, this type of folk religion is Obeah, *Obi*, *Obea* or *Obia* and is derived from the Igbo region of West Africa. In addition to the Caribbean, folk religion has migrated to several American states with large Caribbean populations such as New Orleans, Miami, New York City and Los Angeles.

It is from the legacy of these practices that Caribbean people need deliverance. Although many say they are 'saved', i.e. they confess Jesus as their Lord and Saviour; they are still trapped and affected by the negative affects on the mind of these traditional practices, which those who enforced and practised chattel enslavement passed on from generation to generation ad infinitum. To mitigate against this, we need those who confess to be Christians to renounce all these practices and embrace the liberation and blessings that being in Christ affords. Essentially, they need to undertake a deliverance and healing course. So what is deliverance? Outlined below is a synopsis of the process of deliverance.

An introduction to deliverance from evil spirits

The term "deliverance" as used here encompasses both the process and the result of one's liberation from demonic bondage. Effectively, an evil spirit is holding the individual as an emotional or spiritual captive. We drive out the evil spirits using the authority of the name of the Lord Jesus Christ and thus the individual is 'set free'. Jesus said, "In my name they [believers in Him] will drive out demons" Mark 16:17.

If you are unfamiliar with the scriptural background for deliverance, there are several Christian authors who have written books on aspects of deliverance, including:- Derek Prince, *They Shall Expel Demons*; and *Blessings and Curses*; John Bevere, *The Bait of Satan* and many others.

Deliverance basics

The Gospels of Matthew, Mark and Luke are replete with accounts of Jesus casting demons out of people. As much as one third of Jesus' earthly ministry was devoted to deliverance. His purpose in becoming human, dying on the cross and conquering the grave was to defeat Satan on our behalf. John tells us that this was the reason for Jesus' coming, viz; "The reason the Son of God appeared was to destroy the devil's work", I John 3:8.

The Jewish religious leaders were amazed at the authority Jesus exercised over demons and they said, "He even gives orders to evil spirits and they obey him," Mark 1:27. Jesus did not use incantations or any sort of paraphernalia; he merely spoke to these real yet invisible beings and they obeyed Him. "He drove out the spirits with a word…" Matthew 8.16. Furthermore, Jesus trained the twelve apostles, plus seventy-two other disciples and commissioned them to cast out demons. See Matthew 10:1; Luke 10:1, 17.

Prior to his ascension into heaven, Jesus commissioned his church to preach the Gospel throughout the world, confirming the word with signs, the first of which was deliverance. This involves forcing the demoniacs to depart from a person in the Name of Jesus. So Mark records the following: "And these signs will accompany those who believe, in my name they will drive out demons" Mark 16:15-20.

The Believer's Authority

Christ has entrusted believers with a spiritual "power of attorney"; this is the authority to act in the absence and interests of another. Since all authority in heaven and on earth belongs to Jesus (Matthew 28:18), who delegates his authority and he has given us complete power over Satan and his demonic kingdom. When we cast out demons, the devil has no power to retaliate or harm us in any way. Jesus said: "I have given you authority to trample on snakes and scorpions, and to overcome all the power of the enemy; nothing will harm you," Luke 10:1.

Deliverance is for God's people

When a Gentile woman requested deliverance for her little daughter, Jesus refused her and declared that deliverance is "the children's bread" Matthew 15:26. Only after she expressed faith in Him did he comply with her request. He said, "Woman, you have great faith! Your request is granted" Matthew 15:28. Similarly, everyone else, who through faith in Christ becomes God's children, is qualified to receive 'the children's bread'.

A person who has not acknowledged Jesus Christ as Lord and Saviour does not seek or submit to deliverance. He or she has no interest in the provisions of the cross; their eyes are blind and hearts hardened. They are dead in sins, following the ways of Satan through the ways of this world, since Satan is the 'ruler of the kingdom of the air' (Ephesians 2:1). They cannot benefit from deliverance because without filling themselves with the virtues of the Holy Spirit, the evil spirits could come back seven times stronger than before. "When an evil spirit comes out of a man, it goes through arid places seeking rest and does not find it. Then it says, 'I will return to the house I left.' When it arrives, it finds the house unoccupied, swept clean and put in order. Then it goes and takes with it seven other spirits more wicked than itself, and they go in and live there. And the final condition of that man is worse than the first" Matthew 12:43-45.

Can a Christian have a demon?

No distinction is warranted between Christians and non-Christians having demons; the New Testament makes no such distinction. Our hearts are grieved by those who contend that Christians cannot have demons, thus robbing believers of a valid ministry purchased for us by the blood of Jesus.

Can a Christian be demon possessed?

As a Christian, can I be possessed? Herein lies much of the confusion. "Having" demons and being "possessed" by demons are entirely different matters. Possession denotes ownership. A Christian belongs to Christ. He has been purchased by the precious blood of Jesus (I Corinthians 6: 19-20).

The King James Bible, and a few other versions, have translated the Greek word daimonizomai as "demon possessed", whereas the word specifically means "to act under the control of demons". "Those who were thus afflicted expressed the mind and consciousness of the demon or demons indwelling them" (Vine's Expository Dictionary of New Testament Words). Christians can be influenced and controlled by demons who indwell them, but demons cannot "possess" (own) a Christian. Demons dwelling in Christians are trespassers without ownership rights; therefore, they are subject to eviction in the authority of the Name of the One who has redeemed such believers unto himself by his blood (I Peter 1:18).

Some have questioned, "How can an evil spirit dwell in a person who has the Holy Spirit within him?" The answer is made clear by remembering that, "Your body is a temple of the Holy Spirit" I Corinthians 6: 19. The temple in Jerusalem had three parts: Outer Court, Holy Place and Holy of Holies. The presence of God dwelt solely in the Holy of Holies. The three compartments in the temple correspond to man's tripartite being: body, soul and spirit. For the Christian, the human spirit corresponds to the Holy of Holies, which is the dwelling place of the Holy Spirit. The Holy Spirit desires us to submit every area of our "temple" to His control. Other temple areas include the mind, the emotions, the will and the physical body.

Jesus found defilement in the Jerusalem temple; however, the money changers and the merchants with doves and cattle were not in the Holy of Holies, but in the outer courts of the temple. Jesus proceeded to "cast out" all who defiled the temple (Matthew 21:12). This is a perfect analogy to deliverance. Defilement is not in the spirit of a Christian but in the "outer courts" of his mind, emotions and body. There can be defilement in the Outer Court while the presence of the Lord remains in the Holy of Holies. Jesus is highly displeased with such a condition as he wants his temple cleansed and every defiling demon cast out.

Balance is a key factor

Not every problem is demonic. For example, Jesus healed people without casting out demons. Not every demonic problem is exclusively demonic; there are also fleshly attitudes and activities which must be crucified. Corrupt flesh and unclean spirits are companions; you rarely find one without the other. Anyone who receives valid deliverance cannot expect to retain his deliverance apart from disciplined living. His tongue, mind, emotions, will, physical appetites, finances and his 'spirit-man' must remain rigorously disciplined. "Like a city whose walls are broken down is a man who lacks self-control" Proverbs 25:28. The enemy has ready access to the life of one whose walls of discipline are not solidly constructed.

Why seek deliverance?

Why would a person want deliverance for himself; and is needing relief from torment, defilement, addiction or compulsive behaviour a valid motivation? We know our Lord wants us to be free from all oppressive bondage, so that our highest motivation would be conforming to his likeness. We should hate everything in us that detracts from this process and gives an advantage to the devil.

Prerequisites for deliverance

The word of God lays down three absolute prerequisites for those who seek deliverance from oppressing evil spirits.

First, one must repent of all sin. Repentance is a firm resolve in the Lord to forsake sin and turn about to walk in the ways of God. Ongoing sin in one's life is an open invitation to demons. Yielding to sin is yielding to a "whom", a person: namely, the devil. "Do you not know that to whom you present yourselves slaves to obey, you are the one's slaves whom you obey, whether of sin to death, or of obedience to righteousness?" Romans 6:16.

Second, there must be unqualified forgiveness toward all others no matter what they have done, how many times they have done it, or whether they continue to offend. Forgiveness of oneself is also mandatory. Anyone who has any reservation about forgiving any other person is turned over to tormenting demons until he pays the debt of love's forgiveness. "In anger his master turned him [the unforgiving servant] over to the jailers until he should pay back all he owed. This is how my heavenly Father will treat each of you unless you forgive your brother from your heart" Matthew 18:21-35 (Brackets mine).

Third, there must be a complete separation from every association no matter how casual with the occult, cults and Eastern Religions. This separation includes the destruction of all books and paraphernalia associated therewith. (Deuteronomy 7:25-26; 18:9-13; Acts 19: 19-21).

Judged by its fruit

One day a group of proud, pious Pharisees challenged the validity of Jesus' deliverance ministry. They accused him saying, "It is only by Beelzebub, the prince of demons, that this fellow drives out demons" Matthew 12:24. In the midst of a particularly pointed response, Jesus challenged his critics with these words: "Make a tree good and its fruit will be good, or make a tree bad and its fruit will be bad, for a tree is recognized by its fruit" Matthew 12:33. Indeed, deliverance is a very fruitful ministry. Many people have been set free from bondage in their minds, emotions and physical bodies.

Children in particular need deliverance. Those children who are deemed unruly, once delivered are an amazement to their parents. The child who is not responsive to training, discipline or love, is completely transformed after going through one session of deliverance. The change is the tangible fruit of deliverance!

It is a tremendous benefit to children when, by casting out oppressing demons, those resistant to discipline become pliable; those who could not be cuddled are now receptive to touching love; the rebellious and stubborn become governable; the devious are made trainable in truthfulness and honesty, and the restless and agitated become peaceful. Consider the quality difference that deliverance can make in a person's life.

Each child that is born into this world is a unique individual. God has designed each one with a personality all his or her own. One of the greatest challenges parents face is training and nurturing each child so that the full potential of their special personality is developed and channelled in the ways of God. When evil spirits hinder or block this process, conscientious parents can become perplexed and discouraged. Children are the most valuable assets that a family, church or society has. The objective of Christian parents and ministers should always be to lead children to love and serve Jesus Christ so that they will not be captured by the demonic systems of this world.

If we expect to be free from the oppression of evil spirits, we must engage in spiritual warfare, utilizing every resource that God provides. He counsels us, "Be strong in the Lord and in his mighty power. Put on the full armour of God so that you can take your stand against the devil's schemes" Ephesians 6:10-11.

We have been given three offensive weapons by which to cast out every oppressing spirit: the name of Jesus: "Jesus" is the name of absolute authority. His name is above all other names. The authority of Jesus' name is given to everyone who believes in him for salvation through the forgiveness of sins. Thus, every believer has the right to say to demons, "Go! In the name of Jesus", and the demons must obey.

The power in his blood: The blood that Jesus shed on the cross is incorruptible – it never dies and never loses its power. To use the blood of Jesus as a weapon, tell the devil and his demons what his blood has done for you. It has ransomed, redeemed, atoned, justified and sanctified you.

The word of God: his word is called "the sword of the Spirit" Ephesians 6:17. We use the Word in warfare when we read or quote aloud applicable scriptures to the devil. This is what Jesus did in the time of his wilderness temptations. He said, "Satan, it is written...." In times of battle against the devil, the anointing of the Holy Spirit should be sought and anticipated. The power channels for the Holy Spirit's anointing are the gifts of the Spirit. Of special importance in spiritual warfare is the gift of "discerning of spirits". By means of this gift there comes a supernatural insight in the spiritual realm so that one is able to know the presence, nature and activities of evil spirits. The gift of discerning of spirits guides the deliverance minister in his work. He need not call upon lying spirits to identify themselves, for the Holy Spirit has already revealed to him who they are. (See: Acts 1:8; I Corinthians 12:7-11).

Furthermore, the gift of "faith" arms one with strength to speak to evil spirits with absolute assurance of victory over them. Jesus taught that by speaking in faith one can remove a mountain. Demons indwelling a person represent a mountainous problem that demands removal. The Bible says, "Covet earnestly the best gifts" and "desire spiritual gifts"- I Corinthians 12:31; 14:1.

An effective way to begin a deliverance ministry is for the person seeking deliverance to verbalize specific prayers and confessions. Such prayers will affirm the individual's relationship with Jesus Christ, make definite request of God for deliverance and serve the forces of darkness their eviction notice.

Chapter 7

DELIVERANCE PRAYERS AND CONFESSIONS:

General confession and prayer

"Lord Jesus Christ, I believe that you are the Son of God. You are the Saviour come in the flesh to destroy the works of the devil. You died on the cross for my sins and rose up from the dead. I now confess all of my sins, known and unknown, and repent of each one. I ask you to forgive me and cleanse me in your blood. I do believe that your blood cleanses me now from all sin. Thank you for redeeming me, cleansing me, and sanctifying me in your blood."

Forgiveness prayer

"Lord, others have trespassed against me, but in obedience to your command I now forgive each person who has ever hurt me in any way. As an act of my will I now forgive (name them, both living and dead). Lord, bless each of these; I love them with your love, and I ask you to forgive them also. And since You have forgiven me, I also forgive and accept myself in the name of Jesus Christ. The curse of un-forgiveness has no more power in my life."

Occult confession prayer

"I confess as sin and seek your forgiveness for every occult involvement. I confess having sought from Satan the help that should only come from God. I renounce every occult activity; I renounce Satan and all his works. I loose myself from him, and I take back all the ground I ever yielded to him. I choose the blessing and not the curse. I choose life and not death."

Loosing from domination prayer (breaking soul ties)

"In the name of the Lord Jesus Christ, I now renounce, break and loose myself from all demonic subjection to my mother, my father, my grandparents and any other human beings, living or dead, who have dominated and controlled me in any way. I thank you, Lord, for setting me free."

Psychic heredity and bondage prayer

"In the name of Jesus Christ, I now renounce, break and loose myself and my family from all hereditary curses, and from all demonic bondage placed upon us as the result of sins, transgressions or iniquities through myself, my parents or any of my ancestors. I confess the sins of my forefathers."

Loosing from witchcraft and related powers

"In the name of Jesus Christ I now rebuke, break and loose myself, and my family, from any and all evil curses operating through charms, vexes, hexes, spells, omens, jinxes, psychic powers, mind control, bewitchments, witchcraft or sorcery, that have been put upon me through any person, or from any cult or occult source. I command all such demonic powers to leave me in the name of Jesus. I am the head and not the tail. I am above and not beneath."

Prayer of recognition

"I come to you, Jesus, as my Deliverer. You know all my problems — the things that bind me; that torment me; that defile and harass me. I now loose myself from every dark spirit, from every evil influence, from every satanic bondage, from every spirit in me that is not the Spirit of God, and I command all such spirits to leave me now, in the name of Jesus Christ. I now confess that my body is a temple of the Holy Spirit, redeemed, cleansed and sanctified by the blood of Jesus. Therefore, Satan has no place in me, and no power over me, through the blood of Jesus."

Breaking curses confession

"In the name of Jesus Christ I confess all the sins of my forefathers and by the redemptive blood of Jesus, I now break the power of every curse passed down to me through my ancestral line. I confess and repent of each and every sin that I have committed, known or unknown, and accept Christ's forgiveness. He has redeemed me from the curse of the law. I choose the blessing and reject the curse. In the name of my Lord Jesus Christ, I break the power of every evil curse spoken against me. I cancel the force of every prediction spoken about me, whether intentionally or carelessly, that was not according to God's promised blessings. I bless those who have cursed me. I forgive each person who has ever wronged me or spoken evil of me. In the name of Jesus, I command every evil spirit of curse to leave me now."

Commitment to Christ

"Heavenly Father, I am your child, redeemed by the precious blood of Jesus. You have given me life, and I now give my life to you. My heart's desire is to glorify your

Name. I am an ambassador for Christ and a minister of reconciliation. In your strength I will love, obey and serve you all the days of my life. Amen!"

Bibliography

Appleton, Josie, 'Keeping black boys in the ghetto?', *Spiked On- Line* website (April 2006, http://www.spiked-online.com/Articles/0000000CA92F.htm)

Archer, Coreene, 'Celebrating 21 Years of Service', *Focus: The African and Caribbean Evangelical Alliance*, Nov (2005) 12-13

Beckford, Robert, *Dread and Pentecostal: A Political Theology for The Black Church in Britain*, London: SPCK, 2000

Beckford, Robert, *God and the Gangs*, London: Darton, Longman & Todd, 2004

Beckford, Robert, *Jesus Dub - A Theology of Culture*, London: Routledge, 2005

Beckford, Robert, 'Prophet of Dub: Dub as a Heuristic for Theological Reflection', *Black Theology: An International Journal*, Vol.1 No.1 (2002) 67-82

Boodram, Annan and Muir, John, 'The Dilemma of Being Afro Caribbean in Britain's Schools

Carib Voice website (December 2005, http://www.caribvoice.org/Features/afrocarib.html)

Brown-Douglas, K, *The Black Christ*, New York: Orbis Books, 1994

Buchanan, Emily, 'Black Church Celebrate Growth', *BBC NEWS* website (May 2006, http://news.bbc.co.uk/1/hi/uk/822 200.stm)

Burrow, Rufus. Jr, *James H. Cone and Liberation Theology*, North Carolina: McFarland, 1994

Byfield, Cheron, *Empowering Black Parents to Empower their Sons: A Guide for Black Parents*, Birmingham: The National Black Boys Can Association, 2003

Byron, Naomi, 'Britain's Summer of Discontent' *Socialism Today* website (February 2006, http://www.socialismtoday. org/59/summer.html)

Campbell-Stephens, Rosemary, 'Building a Culture of Success', an unpublished paper presented at the conference: *Building A Culture of Success: Promoting the Achievement of Under-Achieving Groups in Harrow Schools*, London: Harrow Council, March 2006

Casciani, Dominic, 'Street Pastors on a Mission from God', *BBC NEWS* website (April 2006, http://news.bbc.co.uk/1/ hi/uk/2834993.stm)

Channer, Yvonne, *I Am A Promise*, Stoke-on-Trent: Trentham Books, 1995

Chazan, David, "Living god's' funeral divides Rastas', *BBC News Africa* website (May 2006, http://news.bbc.co.uk/1/hi/world/africa/1007894.stm)

Coard, Bernard, How the West Indian Child is Made Educationally Subnormal in the British School System: The Scandal of the Black Child in Schools in Britain, London: New Beacon Books, 1971

Coard, Bernard, 'Thirty Years On: Where Do We Go From Here', in Brian Richardson (eds.), *Tell It Like It Is: How Our Schools Fail Black Children*, Stoke-on-Trent: Trentham Books, 2005, 184-191

Cone, James, H., *A Black Theology of Liberation*, New York: Orbis Books, 1999

Cone, James, H., For My People: Black Theology and the Black Church (The Bishop Henry McNeal Turner Studies in North American Black Religion, Vol1), New York: Orbis Books, 2003

Cone, James H., *God of the Oppressed*, London: SPCK, 1977

Cone, James H., *Risks of Faith: The Emergence of a Black Theology of Liberation, 1968-1998*, Boston: Beacon Press, 1999

Cone, James H., 'Theology's Great Sin: Silence in the Face of White Supremacy' *Black Theology: An International Journal*, Vol.2 No.2 (2004) 139-152

Curtis, Polly, 'Opportunity Locked', *Education Guardian* website (March 2006, http://education.guardian.co.uk/racism/story/0,10795,1402532,00.html)

DfES, *Inclusion: Promoting Inclusion and Tackling Underperformance*, ref. DfES 0063-2005, London: The Stationary Office, 2005

Evans, James, H., *We Have Been Believers*, Minneapolis: Fortress Press 1992

Foster Charles, R., and Smith, Fred, *Black Religious Experience: Conversations on double consciousness and the work of Grant Shockley*, Tennessee: Abingdon Press, 2003

Geer, Sharon, 'The ACE Project: Working successfully to ensure the Attainment of African-Caribbean Boys', in Brian Richardson (eds.), *Tell It Like It Is: How Our Schools Fail Black Children*, Stoke-on-Trent: Trentham Books, 2005, 201-205

Greater London Authority, London Schools and the Black Child II: The Search for Solutions 2003 Conference Report, London: GLA, 2004

Green, Laurie, *Let's Do Theology: a pastoral cycle resource book*, London: Continuum, 2002

Hinds, Gary, 'You've taken my Blues and gone,' on Sounds of Blackness, *The Journey of the Drum*, Minnesota: Townsend Record Label, 1994

Hopkins, Dwight, N., *Black Theology USA and South Africa*, Maryknoll, New York: Orbis Books, 1989

James, Winston, 'Migration, Racism and Identity', in Winston James and Clive Harris (eds.) *Inside Babylon*, London: Verso, 1993

King, Martin Luther , *A Testament of Hope: Essential Writings of*, London/New York: Harper, 1991

King, Martin Luther, *Strength to Love*, London: Collins / Fontana, 1969

Lambeth Council (editors, author unknown), 'Claude Ramsey', in *Many Winters On:*

Memories of Britain's Post War Caribbean Immigrants, London: South London Press, 1998, p.37-40

Mahamdallie, H, 'Is This as Good as it Gets?', in Brian Richardson (eds.), *Tell It Like It Is: How Our Schools Fail Black Children*, Stoke-on-Trent: Trentham Books, 2005, 228-236

McFarlane, Gary, 'A Black Governor's View', in Brian Richardson (eds.), *Tell It Like It Is: How Our Schools Fail Black Children*, Stoke-on-Trent: Trentham Books, 2005, 192-200

Metropolitan Police, 'Operation Trident', *Metropolitan Police Service* website, (May 2006, http://www.met.police.uk/trident/)

National Statistics Online, (Author unknown), *Ethnicity and Identity* website, (Jan 26, 2006, http://www.statistics.gov.uk/ CCI/nugget.asp?ID=1388&Pos=1&ColRank=2&Rank= 144)

Northrup, David, (ed.) *The Atlantic Slave Trade*, Lexington, MA: DC Heath Co., 1994, 12-35

OFSTED, Achievement of Black Caribbean Pupils: Good Practice in Secondary Schools, HMI 448, London: HMSO, 2002

Philips, Mike & Philips, Trevor, *Windrush: The Irresistible Rise of Multi-Racial Britain*, London: Harper Collins, 1999

Rampton, A, West Indian Children in our Schools: Interim Report of the Committee of Inquiry into the Education of Children from Ethnic Minority Groups, CMD 273, London: MHSO, 1981

Reddie, Anthony, *From Nobodies to Somebodies*, Peterborough: Epworth Press, 2003

Reddie, Anthony, *Growing into Hope: Believing and Expecting*, Peterborough: Epworth Press, 1998

Select Committee, *Race Relation and Immigration*, London: HMSO, 1973

Sewell, Tony, *Black Masculinities and Schooling*, Stoke-on-Trent: Trentham Books, 1997

Simon, David, 'Education of the Blacks: The Supplementary School Movement', in Brian

Richardson (eds.), *Tell It Like It Is: How Our Schools Fail Black Children*, Stoke-on-Trent: Trentham Books, 2005, 64-71

Stone, Maureen, *The Education of the Black Child*, London: Fontana Press, 1981

Sturge, Mark, Look What The Lord Has Done: An Exploration of Black Christian Faith in Britain, Milton Keynes: Scripture Union, 2005

Swann, M, Education for All: The Report of the Committee of Enquiry into the Education of Children from Ethnic Minority Groups, CMD 9453, London: HMSO, 1985

Taylor, Amina, 'Someone To Look Up To', *Education Guardian* website (April 2006, http://www.guardian.co.uk/comment/story/0,3604,1135431,00.html)

Truth and Reconciliation Commission, 'PROMOTION OF NATIONAL UNITY AND RECONCILIATION ACT', 1995', website (March 1st 2006 http://www.doj.gov.za/trc/)

West, Cornell, *Race Matters*, Boston: Beacon Press, 1993

Wilmore, Gayraud. S., Black Religion and Black Radicalism: An Interpretation of the Religious History of African Americans, Revised 3rd Edn, Maryknoll, New York: Orbis Books, 1998

Wimberley, Anne, In Search of Wisdom: Faith Formation in the Black Church. Nashville:

Abingdon Press, 2003

Wimberley, Anne E. Streaty, ed. Keep It Real: Working with Today's Black Youth. Nashville: Abingdon Press, 2005

Wimberley, Anne, *Nurturing Faith and Hope: Black Worship As a Model for Christian Education*. Cleveland: Pilgrim Press, 2004

Wu, Stephen, 'Legal Ramblings' *Creative Common Sense* website (February 2006, http://www.scwu.com/news/static/102021496024297.shtml)

Index